Traditional
Witchcraft
for Urban
Living

Traditional Witchcraft for Urban Living

Mélusine Draco

MOON BOOKS

Winchester, UK
Washington, USA

First published by Moon Books, 2012
Moon Books is an imprint of John Hunt Publishing Ltd., Laurel House, Station Approach,
Alresford, Hants, SO24 9JH, UK
office1@o-books.net
www.o-books.com

For distributor details and how to order please visit the 'Ordering' section on our website.

Text copyright: Mélusine Draco 2009

ISBN: 978 1 84694 978 4

A CIP catalogue record for this book is available from the British Library.

Design: Tom Davies

Printed in the UK by CPI Antony Rowe
Printed in the USA by Offset Paperback Mfrs, Inc

We operate a distinctive and ethical publishing philosophy in all
areas of our business, from our global network of authors to
production and worldwide distribution.

CONTENTS

Traditional Witchcraft for Urban Living is dedicated to all those friends, past and present, with whom I have journeyed part of the way.
Thanks for the memories …

Chapter One – A Pagan Perspective

If much of today's pagan propaganda is to be believed, anyone who doesn't live a stone's throw from, or have regular access to the rural heartlands of England, is hardly qualified to call themselves 'pagan'. And if the unfortunate town-dweller can't be found at weekends rooting about in country hedgerows, then 'witch' is also a label to which they apparently have no right!

Tosh, tosh! And thrice tosh!

Yes, of course, we can haul out the old chestnut of 'pagan' deriving from the Latin *pagus*, which properly means 'belonging to a village' but it was used in a derogative sense, just as contemporary town dwellers might refer to country folk as 'swede bashers' or 'carrot crunchers'. Long after the Christian Church was first established in the cities and towns (centres of learning), what they saw as idolatrous practices continued to be observed in rural districts and villages, so 'pagan' and 'villager' came to mean the same thing. Similarly, the word 'heathen' (from the Anglo-Saxon *hæthen*, *hæth*) referred to a 'dweller on a heath or common'. Christian doctrine would not have reached these remote people until long after it had integrated town and city, and in both cases, 'pagan' and 'heathen' implied a lack of worldliness, sophistication and learning. It was intended as an insult.

In contemporary society, 'pagan' is now the accepted umbrella term for those who follow any eclectic, reconstructionalist doctrines of pre-Christian beliefs, while 'heathen' tends to refer more specifically to those of the revivalist Norse traditions. Ironically, the vast majority of followers of both traditions live in towns and cities. And let's face it, people live in urban communities for a variety of reasons: the most common being the close proximity to work and/or family.

For the witch whose career confines them to an urbanised environment, regular Craft practice may often seem like a futile gesture, especially if home is a small, gardenless-flat. Even the suburbs can be magically incapacitating, if there is constant noise from traffic and neighbours. People work long hours; often setting off for work and getting home again in the dark during the winter months, without having the opportunity to notice the subtle changing of the seasons. Weekends are a constant battle with family commitments, domestic chores and socialising. It's no wonder that the urban witch has little time or strength left for magical and spiritual development.

There are, of course, others who find themselves having to remain town and house-bound because of age or disability; because they are caring for an aged/infirm parent, or partner; or because they have small children. Urbanisation often provides on-the-spot facilities to make things easier on the domestic front but it cannot give the one thing that a witch needs most – privacy and spiritual elbow-room.

So how do we manage?

We get up close and personal. And we reject the textbook clichés of what is, and what is not, recommended witchcraft practice. We do not follow stereotyping when it comes to when, where and how we perform our rituals simply because it may not be practically possible to follow the instructions to the letter.

For example:

I am a Welsh witch and I come from a place midway between the mountains and the sea, but I have not lived in my homeland now for many years. It would be untrue to say that I never experience what the Welsh call *hiraethus*, that indescribable feeling of longing and home-sickness, but as we all know, in magical terms there is always a price to be paid for our Craft. During those long years, my career and domestic life has taken me to London (where I lived for 20 years), to the industrial Midlands and, more recently, to a totally urbanised area of East Anglia. Not once, in all that time did I have the luxury of wild, open spaces – it was all concrete and asphalt. *But not once, in all that time, did I stop being a* real *witch.*

In my experience, the greatest problem a solitary urban witch faces is that an urban environment is not user-friendly when it comes to psychic activity, but then we don't always have a choice of where we are going to live if someone else's needs have to be catered for, too. Mostly I have been confined to renting small terraced cottages and flats, often with little or no garden to give that extra bit of space. I make this comment merely to demonstrate that my Craft activities have not been conducted in a round of luxurious city apartments and picturesque Grade II listed town houses!

Under these circumstances, for me the key words have always been: **acclimatise, adapt** and **improvise.** Any animal, plant or person that is uprooted and transported to another environment quickly learns to acclimatise if it is going to survive. I have adapted to my surroundings and drawn on whatever material/energy there is to hand, even if it is not what I've been used to working with. I improvise by drawing on existing knowledge and experience. So …

Acclimatise:

Accustom yourself to tuning-in to your environment, even if you've lived there for some time. Try to imagine visiting the place for the first time. Buy a detailed street map or guidebook, and familiarise yourself with all the hidden nooks and crannies in the immediate vicinity. Is there a park nearby? Public gardens? Churchyard? Cemetery? What trees are growing locally? Which are the most important/attractive buildings?

Where is the nearest river or canal? Where is the oldest church? Take your time ... explore ... *rediscover* ... **acclimatise**.

Adapt:

Modify or adjust the way you look at things. There is no point in wishing you were elsewhere when circumstances dictate that you remain where you are. But on the other hand there's nothing quite so mind-numbing as doing the same thing, day in day out, for weeks on end. For a change, try walking to the shops, school, or travelling to work, via a different route. Examine what's growing in all the front gardens along the way to the shop, school, station or bus stop. Make sure you take time out for lunch - and get out of the home or working environment for an hour - even if it's a wet Wednesday afternoon: after all, a witch shouldn't be afraid of a little drop of Elemental Water! Start seriously interacting with your environment ... *adapt*.

Improvise:

Be prepared to perform a magical working at any time, without preparation, and without what is considered to be the 'proper regalia'. Be aware of the magical signs Nature has to offer and be ready to act spontaneously, even in the middle of a crowded railway station or shopping mall during rush hour! It may also come as a bit of a shock to realise that a large number of books mentioned in this text are *not* about witchcraft, or written by witches. This is because we are learning to *improvise* and look at things from a different or unexpected perspective.

Before we go out and meet Nature face to face, however, there may be one or two changes needed to enable us to re-connect with the natural, elemental energies that are an essential ingredient within any magical environment. Sorry ... we're not talking about symbolic bowls of water, salt, night-lights and a joss stick to mark the quarters on the sitting room rug, we're talking about encountering *real* Elemental Air, *real* Elemental Water, *real*

Elemental Earth and *real* Elemental Fire - up close and personal!

Elemental Air:

This is ... wait for it ... *fresh air*! It's the stuff every living thing on the planet needs to breathe to stay alive but, apart from the occasional jaunt to a pagan camp, a large number of urban pagans appear to be terrified of it. I've been into some homes where the stuffy, cluttered atmosphere is so over-powering that you could cut the reek of stale incense with a knife. Whilst we appreciate that modern society no longer allows us to live with our doors and windows wide open, we must get used to letting cleansing air back into our lives. There *is* a purifying element to fresh air!

In both religious and magical terms, however, Elemental Air is usually represented by smoke from the incense carrying our prayers and entreaties up to the gods. As Joules Taylor observes in *Perfume Power*, the burning of fragrance to represent questions or appeals is an ancient and well-nigh indestructible facet of worship. In other words, from very early times fragrance has been associated with the gods, the soul and spiritual qualities. Learn to recognise *natural* fragrance (not always pleasant) from the world around you, and not to rely totally on the contrived atmospherics of the incense burner!

As Jules Taylor goes on to observe, our once highly developed sense of smell is now generally under deployed and now perhaps the least-regarded of all human senses. We *can* improve our 'scent perception' by simply concentrating on becoming more aware of the smells around us. Unfortunately, the urban witch also has to contend with exhaust fumes, fast-food outlets and all manner of other municipal pollution, but with practice it *is* possible to detect the faint fragrance of Nature. If we want to reconnect with Nature the first thing we must do is sharpen our senses and learn to read the signs that come to us on the breeze.

Elemental Air brings lightness and freedom of spirit, as well as being a universal symbol of irresistible force and uncontrollable power.

Exercise:

In town it's often difficult to find a moment, or even a place to relax. In the larger towns and cities the noise is a constant, 24-hour drone of traffic, where people never seem to sleep. With the use of a local map, find a 'green spot' ... even if it's only a small churchyard or square ... where you can sit, watch and listen.

Okay, but what are we watching and listening for?

Nature ... because she is there all around us, all the time. For example, I've encountered a green woodpecker while sitting in the small courtyard garden of a coffee shop in the middle of town. I've seen (and heard) hundreds of these birds over the years, but this was the closest I'd ever been ... just five feet away. How many different birds (most certainly creatures of Elemental Air) can *you* identify? If the answer is very few, then how can you hope to begin to read those 'signs' that make up a large part of the witch's world?

Invest a few coppers in a book on British birds from a local charity shop, or buy off e-bay, or ABE-Books on the Internet. Start learning, even if it's only by watching the pigeons in Trafalgar Square! You'll be surprised how many different birds can be spotted in our towns and inner cities on a regular basis, and birds have been always been considered bearers of omens since ancient times.

Elemental Water:

Water is the essential ingredient of life but how many of us consciously pay homage to this fact in our day-to-day existence? We use water for the daily ritual cleansing of our home and body, to water the garden or wash the car, but often neglecting its spiritual properties. From prehistoric times, our ancestors considered springs and 'watery places' to be sacred, and the contemporary custom of throwing coins into wells and municipal fountains goes back to the times when votive offerings were cast into the waters to propitiate the gods. We should be mindful that water, particularly spring water, is truly a 'gift of the gods' and not to be treated casually.

For magical purposes we need to re-connect with water, for even the most rubbish-clogged urban watercourse carries life-giving properties along its muddy artery. If we live close to a river, canal, park or golf course, then it makes it easier to observe water at close quarters during the changing seasons, and come to recognise the local wildlife that depends on it. Even the modern fountain in the city centre can be a focus for meditative moments when the sun catches the colours of the rainbow in the falling spray.

Our local brook regularly acts as a depository for shopping trolleys, traffic cones and other domestic debris, as it runs right through the centre of town. Growing through the restraining brickwork, however, is a magnificent elder tree and an amazing collection of harts-tongue ferns, which I haven't seen in such profusion since leaving Wales. Most days the flow is the barest trickle but when it rains, the watercourse becomes a raging torrent. The only other 'watery' place is the dried bed of an old pond that only floods during the winter months, but this is the *real* magical place. The water has gone because the surrounding urban development has drained it, but the site is old, with a large stand of reed mace and a host of other interesting creatures living in this well-established habitat.

There are numerous ideas for a 'water feature' in the home, and much depends on personal taste rather than pagan cliché. Even the smallest courtyard can host an ornamental wall fountain, birdbath or wooden barrel containing miniature water lilies (although these do require direct sunlight for success). Inside, a large bowl with flower heads floating on the surface can be extremely attractive ... but not a good idea if you have small children or a large dog. Be creative, use your imagination.

Elemental Water 'saturates our lives and language and is the most compelling of human metaphors' wrote Rebecca Rupp in *Four Elements*; it is the universal symbol of primal mystery.

Exercise:

Trace your local source of natural water and try to follow it for as far as possible.

You may be lucky enough to live near a pond, stream, lake, river or canal and can watch the changing face of the seasons at the water margin. How many different species of flora and fauna dependent on an Elemental Water habitat can *you* identify? If the answer is very few, then how can you hope to begin to read those 'signs' that make up a large part of the witch's world?

Remember that pure (or purified) water is sterile and that for magical purposes we need to work with *natural* water. Unless you have access to a spring or holy-well, place a wide bowl or jar outside on a window-sill, to catch rain or moisture; transfer to a sealable bottle and keep for use in your rites. But don't drink rainwater!

Elemental Earth:

Of all the elements, Earth is the symbol of solidity and substance, and the 'most intrusive in our daily lives', was an observation made by Rebecca Rupp. The subject of global warming and saving the planet is at the forefront of everyone's mind these days, but for the witch, the sanctity of the Earth and Nature has *always* been paramount. The witch does not 'worship' Nature but exists in a sort of 'spiritual care-taking' capacity – after all, it is from Nature direct that we divine the signs and symbols that give us the power over natural things.

Communing with Nature isn't always easy in an urban environment and it is very often necessary to 'manufacture' a moment of peace for ourselves amongst the busy populace. Dig out a copy of that famous junior school poem by William Henry Davies, 'Leisure' that begins: *"What is this life if, full of care, We have no time to stand and stare ... "* and take a verse for your very own Thought for the Day. Without compromising your personal safety, try to visit the local park or old cemetery during school hours, or early on a weekend morning, when you can guarantee having a quiet corner to yourself for a while.

Many years ago, long before the 'great clean up' got underway, we lived near Highgate Cemetery and this was a perfect place for a meditative or magical moment. The magnificent monuments were overgrown and apart from the occasional tourist visit at weekends, we pretty much had the place to ourselves via a discreet hole in the boundary fence. Not only had Nature taken over completely and the place full of wildlife, but there was also the comfortable familiarity that all witches should have with both the spirits of the dead, and the spirits of Nature.

But how do we bring Elemental Earth into our urban home? By growing something, of course! Not everyone has green fingers but it doesn't take much effort to introduce a small selection of supermarket-grown potted herbs to the kitchen window-sill, does it? This small gesture gives a dual sense of purpose, in that we are caring for something that we can utilise in our day-to-day cooking and magic. Go one better and buy a small kitchen bay. As well as having culinary uses, bay is one of the oldest sacred herbs with strong protective powers when used in spell-casting. My bay started out (many years ago) some six inches high and now stands three-foot tall in a large pot that can be transported anywhere. This is your first step in learning (or re-learning) about wort-lore within the confines of urbanity.

Elemental Earth gives a feeling of security. Universal myths claim that first man was created out of clay, earth or sand; traditionally Earth is represented by the 'mother' and the harvest.

Exercise:

It must be obvious that Elemental Earth is much more complex than we would first imagine. We live on it, our food comes from it, we bury our dead in it, Elemental Earth (North) is the direction of magical Power ... and yet most of us are afraid of getting our hands dirty by interacting with it. So now is the time to re-discover the Earth energies around where you live, by going out and making time to stand and stare!

This also time for an exercise in personal honesty; be truthful, just how comfortable are *you* with quiet corners of a park or cemetery? If the answer is 'not very', then how can you hope to begin to read those spiritual and temporal 'signs' that make up a large part of the witch's world? Again, I would repeat, never compromise your personal safely while on your quest, but try to determine whether you are nervous because you feel vulnerable (i.e. alone), or whether you are uncomfortable with the close proximity to the natural (and supernatural) worlds.

Elemental Fire:

In its natural state, Elemental Fire is the most elusive of the four within an urban environment, unless the local vandals have ignored the ASBO and gone on a car-torching spree! Fire has always played an important part in esoteric gatherings but the historic concept of a coven gathering around the bonfire in a woodland clearing is highly suspect. A single candle flame can be seen for miles on a dark night, and in the days when witches were falling foul of the law, a blazing fire would have been an open invitation to the Witch Finders. Fire, however, is part of the Mysteries of Craft and an integral part of any magical working.

First man probably encountered fire as the result of a lightning strike, and so he would have been left in no doubt that the resulting blaze was indeed heaven-sent. From that time to the present, that god-gift of heat and light has provided the dual-purpose of hearth fire (domestic) and sacred flame (religious) ... *both equally as important as a spiritual focus.* For our purposes the hearth-fire is, of course, the most obvious, for witches require no formal temples or sanctuaries in order to follow their Craft.

Our urban problem of fire lighting was solved by purchasing a circular patio heater – this is a domed-mesh cover affair, with a tray underneath to catch hot ash so it can safely be used on decking – and also doubles as a barbeque. It can be used in confined spaces and moved to another home when necessary. We also have a collection of old-fashioned lanterns (probably nearer the true), which double up for both indoor and outdoor working ... and infinitely safer than naked candles.

Elemental Fire is the symbol of warmth, passion ... and danger. It can offer the welcome of a glowing hearth or an uncontrollable conflagration that destroys everything in its path. Those who pass through the flames and survive, emerge transformed and improved.

Exercise:
Learn to love fire and make a point of always having a candle burning (safely) while you are at home. Treat yourself to a 'special' holder that will always act as the focus for your devotions – whether indoors or out – so think in terms of something generous, expensive and wind-proof, like a storm-lantern. If you are fortunate enough to have a patio heater or an open fire, buy some of those wonderful copper sulphate- coated pinecones that produce the most amazing coloured flames - perfect for divination - but don't cook over them! Now ... how comfortable are *you* with fire? If the answer is 'not very', then

how can you hope to begin to read those divinatory 'signs' that make up a large part of the witch's world?

Important: When out and about, never put yourself at risk by wandering in remote places. More attacks on lone people occur in urban areas rather than out in the countryside, so do not be foolhardy – *the gods do not always protect.*

We also need to accept that witchcraft (unlike Wicca) is *not* a religion – it never has been, simply because it's an individual's *natural ability* that distinguishes him or her as a witch. In other words, a witch is born, not made. It just isn't possible to learn how to become a witch if we haven't got these abilities, although it *is* possible to learn how to hone and develop latent, or suppressed psychic talents, under the right tuition. And there is no age limit for these discoveries – in either the young, middle-aged or old.

Wicca, on the other hand, is fast becoming accepted as the 'new pagan religion' with its doctrines drawing heavily on an eco-feminine shadow-image of Christianity. This again is nothing new, since Christianity itself absorbed many of the existing pagan festivals and celebrations into the Church calendar (including an identification of the Virgin Mary with Isis), and contemporary paganism is merely reclaiming its own. But in reality, even in the days before the Christian invasion, not all of the pagan populace were skilled in the Craft of witches.

To use a natural analogy, the differences between witchcraft and paganism *per se* is to liken them to the relationship between the domestic and the wild cat. To the casual observer there is little difference. Just as the similarities between the modern wild cat (*felis sylvestris*) and the house cat (*felis catus*) are so great and the differences so few, that it is difficult to establish any authentic genealogy. There is evidence that wild cats have mated with domestic cats and domestic cats can survive in the wild having gone feral, but they don't usually move far from human habitation and will quickly revert if given the opportunity. The wild cat, however, cannot be handled or tamed; even a small kitten it is extremely ferocious. In appearance it is difficult at a distance to distinguish a wild cat from a large domestic tabby that has gone feral, but (as with witchcraft and paganism), the subtle differences *are* there, if you know where and *how* to look. For example:

Paganism (including Wicca) has developed a very strong community spirit in recent years, with everyone at public events joining hands to celebrate the festivals, organised around the nearest weekend coinciding with a formal Wheel of the Year. Pagans believe that information should be available to all, and that everyone has the right to access all esoteric knowledge. Many pagans are highly suspicious of witches and some will deny that they practice any form of magic at all. Paganism caters for teenagers within the community and actively encourages them to attend the fairs, buy the books and any appropriate accoutrements. Pagans claim to worship Nature in the persona of 'the Goddess'.

The generally accepted pagan motto is: 'And it harm none, do what you will'.

Witchcraft is not bound by social rules and conventions, only by *the personal morality of the individual,* and is governed solely by the natural tides. Any form of magical working or spiritual observance tends to be of a solitary nature, or in the company of tried and trusted people. Witches believe that esoteric knowledge should be kept hidden because it is impossible to convey the meaning of the 'true mysteries' without the appropriate teaching. Traditional witches are now rarely seen at pagan events, and hold that any ritual equipment will be acquired as and when it is necessary. The witch learns his or her Craft along the way, and pays *homage* to Nature but in a more abstract form that the textbooks will allow, something along the lines of Blake's *Auguries of Innocence:*

> *"To see a World in a grain of sand,*
> *And a Heaven in a flower,*
> *Hold Infinity in the palm of your hand*
> *And Eternity in an hour"*

The witches' motto is 'Trust None!' although it could well be taken from the motto of several Scottish clans: 'Touch not the [wild] cat without a glove'.

Which path will you ultimately tread?

Chapter Two - The Unofficial Countryside

When Richard Mabey wrote the Prologue of his excellent book *The Unofficial Countryside*, he shared a few thoughts and observations that many frustrated urban witches today would recognise. The bad day at work; the petty grievances of colleagues; the stifling atmosphere; and the filmy view from too small, grimy windows; followed by a 'creeping three-lane traffic jam' would be enough to dampen even the most resilient of spirits. On impulse he headed down a winding suburban lane that led to a labyrinth of disused gravel pits and reservoirs. It was a far from inspiring place, with the land contaminated by rubbish and dumped cars but in the mood he was in, *"... just to have seen some murky water lapped by non-air-conditioned wind would have set me right ..."*

How often have we found ourselves in that self-same frame of mind, when we feel that the only antidote would be to get out among green fields and woods? We know that nothing is a substitute for the real countryside but we need something to 'earth' the frustration. Richard Mabey goes stomping off along the towpath in a 'black frame of mind' but suddenly he's confronted by the fact that Nature is teeming in the brutalised landscape. *"... the canal here was as clear as a chalk stream. Yellow water lilies drooped like balls of molten wax on the surface. Near the edge of the water drifts of newly hatched fish hung in the shallows ..."*

The writer's narrative unfolds almost like a pathworking as his 'nervous gallop' turns into a stroll and his eyes and mind begin to relax. He is sharing with us his discovery of Nature in unexpected places and under unusual conditions. The flighting swallows swooping low over the water, drawing his eye to the brilliant spikes of purple loosestrife and wine-tinted agrimony blooming all along the tow-path. *"As dusk fell ... I went off home like a new man."*

When the urban blues take over, an excursion such as the one described above can have the desired effect, and serve to 'beat off the urban stresses in their own territory and on their own terms'. Unfortunately, most of us don't look upon inner-city wastelands as a meeting place with Nature. But the meeting places *are* there. As I write, I'm watching a blackbird enjoying a light shower of rain as it sits in a sallow tree that has grown up between our courtyard wall and the racing stable next door. The leaf-less branches are covered in shimmering droplets as the weak winter sun breaks briefly from behind a cloud. A truly magical moment found in the centre of a busy town.

In fact, a crack in the pavement or wall will provide enough space for a plant to flourish and, providing a site has not been contaminated, there is scarcely a nook or cranny that does not offer a home to some species of flora or fauna. Even the most desolate of urban landscapes will often support a wider variety of wildlife than is found in many rural areas. The next time you travel by train or tube (and are fortunate enough to get a window seat), use the opportunity to spot the different plants that are growing in the most unlikely places. Train lines cut through miles of inner-city sprawl and from this vantage point we can get a panoramic view of abandoned water-logged wharfs, defunct railway cuttings, isolated stands of hawthorn blossoming at the edge of industrial estates, overgrown allotments, and the remnants of old woodland clinging desperately to the sides of motorways.

This is the urban witch's world but not everyone is able to identity the plants, or be familiar with their place in traditional wort-lore. It is also difficult to know which are long-established varieties, and which are relatively recent escapees from city gardens.

For example, I once overheard some 'knowledgeable' traveller identifying the profuse growth of buddleia (butterfly bush) along the inner-city rail-tracks as rosebay willowherb. Whilst the former is a garden shrub with no known medicinal properties, the latter 'weed' was recorded in *The Herball* [1597] as follows:

"The branches come out of the ground in great numbers, growing to the height of sixe foote, garnished with brave flowers of great beautie, consisting of fower leaves a piece, or an orient purple colour. The cod is long … and full of downie matter, which flieth away with the winde when the cod is opened."

It might be a good idea to begin by identifying what we mean by 'wort-lore', because there is no standard definition of 'a herb'. Some will say that any useful plant is a herb; others only consider those used for culinary purposes deserve such recognition. Be that as it may, we have a long history of herbal practice in these islands, and not all who believed in the healing power of plants were witches. For example, we have the famous Physicians of Myddfai, who were said to have Faere Folk ancestry, and who passed healing knowledge down from generation to generation for many hundreds of years. Aelfric, a Benedictine monk of Cerne Abbas compiled in both Old English and Latin [995CE], his *Colloquy (Nominum Herbarum)*, listing over 200 plants and trees used for medicinal treatments. Not to mention the 17th century's Nicholas Culpeper, who administered to the poor, preferring to use native plants rather than imported exotics and who would often refer his patients to the nearby countryside where the appropriate herbs could be collected for free.

Throughout the ages herbs have been grown for many purposes and the gift of healing (herbal or otherwise) is obviously a *natural* one. Probably most of those who faced the noose accused of witchcraft, were no more than simple healers with an understanding of potions made from plant extract. In *The Physicians of Myddfai*, Dr Harold Selcon records that by the end of the 14th century a different class of medical herbalists was developing – the apothecaries – who purchased herbs collected from the countryside by wandering herb collectors (the 'green men and women').

The apothecaries might buy the goods to pass on to their town-dwelling customers, but it was the 'green men and women' who knew what to collect, and when. And this is the important part of Craft wort-lore. It isn't enough to know that moneywort can be used in as lotion and applied to wounds, or that a teaspoon of dried cowslip flowers taken as a tea will prevent insomnia. It is also necessary to learn *when* to collect them; *how* to prepare the plants; *what* to mix with them and in what quantity, before they can be of genuine, practical use.

Nevertheless, apart from Culpeper, researchers have largely ignored our native domestic plant medicine, and some of the everyday remedies still used by our great-grandparents are in danger of disappearing altogether. As Gabrielle Hatfield points out in *Memory, Wisdom & Healing: The History of Domestic Plant Medicine*, our traditional domestic plant medicine was a family's first aid kit, that had been handed down through generations with remarkable accuracy. These 'old wives' cures' were preserved in the country well into the 20th century but declined after that when family groups split up and the children moved away. Hatfield also claims that elderly country people who possessed such knowledge would probably have refrained from passing it on to the next generation of town-based off-spring for fear of being ridiculed. Before herbal medicine became fashionable again, hanging on to Granny's old-fashioned remedies would have been seen as 'uncool' to the next generation of urbanites.

Another problem that faces today's urban witch, however, is that unlike her country cousin, it is not advisable to utilise Nature's local available bounty due to the high level of municipal pollution. There may be suitable plants in profusion on urban waste ground and open verges, such as common plantain and horsetail, but all will be coated with industrial and vehicle emissions, dust, grime ... not to mention the gallons of dog pee emptied over them in a growing season!

So this is where we take a leaf [!] out of our medieval predecessors' book and buy what we need from an appropriate outlet. Invest in a serious herbal, such as the *RHS Encyclopaedia of Herbs and Their Uses* and a more relaxed classic like *Culpeper's Colour Herbal*. Use them to make comparisons between 17th century cures and those in use today – simply because the old urban witch would have had to keep up with the trends of the time, and would probably have been a lot more progressive in her thinking than her rural counterparts. Not to mention, that in all honesty, it was more than likely that the wort-lore of country Craft would have stagnated, simply because it was mainly an oral tradition passed from one generation to the next, and not often recorded for posterity.

Exercise:

For the witch, herbs have both a practical (i.e. medicinal) and a magical usage, and we need to build up a supply of those we are most likely to need for our own personal use. For example, I always keep a bottle of witch hazel (bought from Boots!) in the kitchen for treating small burns from the iron or splashes of hot cooking oil. Apply immediately and the burn is cooled and rarely blisters. Cabbage leaves are perfect for drawing splinters, boils and sceptic wounds, while camomile teabags are at hand for a relaxing nightcap before going to bed. Not to mention Bach's rescue remedy for relieving stress. Utilising these simple remedies is so automatic that I never think of them as anything special ... *but they are all old herbal remedies.*

Medicinal

The majority of herbs recommended for home use are considered safe for simple remedies but even these should only be bought from a reputable source. The most common techniques for wort-preparation at home are infusions, decoctions, tinctures, poultices or compresses. Both fresh and dried herbs can be used to make a range of home herbals and although fresh plants have greater medicinal value, dried herbs are available all year round from health food shops. For the beginner, buying herbs in their dried form greatly reduces the chances of taking the wrong herb or dosage. Dried herbs generally lose their potency after 6-7 months, while roots, bark and seeds can be kept for up to three years.

An **infusion** is made in the same way as a pot of tea; strained through a muslin sieve and drunk while hot. The standard dosage for a herbal infusion is one tea cup three times a day. Tea made with camomile (bags) for sleep, or hot honey and lemon juice for a cold, comes under this heading. **Decoctions** are made when roots or the hard woody parts of the plant are used and merely pouring boiling water over the herb is not sufficient to extract the active ingredient. Allow to simmer for at least 20 minutes and strain through a nylon sieve while hot. If kept in a cool place, a decoction will last a day or two. The standard dosage is one teacup three times a day. Unpleasant tasting infusions or decoctions can be sweetened with honey. Although both are usually taken orally, they can also be used in a bath, footbath, as a face wash or hair rinse. Witch hazel for burns comes under this latter heading.

Tinctures contain the active ingredient of a herb in alcohol – the most famous being 'rescue remedy'. Tinctures are often preferred to infusions and decoctions because they are more palatable and, after the initial preparation, are quick and easy to use since they can be taken neat or with a little water. When under stress, take three drops of 'rescue remedy' in a cup of tea. Make a standard tincture with one pint of at least 30% proof alcohol (vodka is ideal), and pour over 4 ounces of dried herbs. Keep the mixture in a warm place for two weeks and shake daily.

Strain the liquid through muslin into a dark, airtight bottle and take 1 teaspoon three times a day. As far as I am concerned, my sloe gin also falls into this category because of the feel-good-factor it produces after one small glass!

Compresses and **poultices** are applied to the outside of the body and are used to treat wounds, skin conditions and strains. A compress is usually applied cold (i.e. a bag of frozen peas for bringing out a bruise, or a cold teabag for tired eyes), whilst a poultice is applied as hot as bearable (for drawing a splinter). A cloth soaked in an infusion or decoction can be used for headaches, and a piece of cabbage leaf (held in place with a plaster) will also draw a splinter or bring a nasty spot to a head. Wounds that are taking their time to heal will usually react to a small poultice of bruised comfrey leaves.

Needless to say, there are thousands of herbal remedies and hundreds of books written on the subject. The above are just a handful of my own tried and trusted remedies that are always on hand in the kitchen. Resist the urge to rush out and stock up your store cupboard with the entire range from Holland & Barrett; begin with one remedy or multi-purpose herb at a time. Experiment and get a *feel* for the plant or ingredients, so that you don't have to *think* about preparation – it comes naturally. One book I would recommend as a starter is *Vinegar, Honey & Garlic: Nature's Secret Weapon* by Maxwell Stein. This little volume looks at vinegar as a condiment, preservative, cleanser and medicament; the benefits of a daily intake of honey, and the amazing properties of garlic – and should be on every urban witch's kitchen shelf.

Magical

When using herbs within magical working or spell-craft, we need to understand exactly what lies behind the superstition and folk-lore surrounding each individual plant, and identify its magical correspondences and planetary associations. For example:

- The folk-lore attached to garlic dates back thousands of years and crosses the world as a means of protection against 'evil spirits' while according to Culpeper, the herb is 'owned' by Mars.

- Culpeper also writes of the bay that it is a "tree of the Sun and under the celestial sign of Leo and resisteth witchcraft very potently, as also all the evils old Saturn can do the body of man, and they are not a few."

Here we are looking at two different levels of potency in protective measures and this is a much more important aspect for the urban witch to learn than for her country counterpart. Living among a higher density of humanity (with all its attendant problems), we are less likely to need protection from psychic attack, and more against the pervading influence of negative energy that is found in concentrated pockets nowadays in all our towns and cities. Even if we keep ourselves aloof from the increasing crime/drink/drugs culture, any neighbouring social malaise can still seriously affect us on a psychic level.

For the urban witch who wishes to work on the astral in the privacy of his/her own home, the protective measures must be **doubled** to ensure that no negative energy is allowed to penetrate our defences. Our Circle must be impenetrable and when we close down after a working, it is essential that no part of the ritual be left undone. I'm always hearing from wanna-be witches that they are exhausted from persistent psychic attack but more often than not, the problem is that their defences have been breached by negative energy due to insufficient preparation, and a degree of arrogance that nothing can harm them. Perhaps because they don't really believe that magic works! Over a period of time, a build-up of localised negative energy *can* develop a life-force of its own, and the only way for it to 'feed' in order to metamorphose, is to latch on to an unsuspecting novice in much the same way as any earthly parasite.

Starting from scratch, we need to cleanse the whole house or flat using a decoction of either garlic or bay, as prepared above. The jury is out as to which of the two is the most powerful but speaking from experience, my money is on the bay. Using the whole of the plant where possible (leaves, stalk, flowers), prepare sufficient liquid to cleanse every entrance to your home – doors, windows, chimney and even air-bricks! Add a tablespoon of salt to the liquid and wipe round the window and door frames; sprinkling any other area such as the fireplace and air-bricks as an added precaution.

This genuine 17th century spell is quite effective for this kind of work, although it does require one or two more active ingredients, which are self-explanatory:

The Spell

Holy water come and bring;
Cast in salt for seasoning;
Set the brush for sprinkling;
Sacred spittle bring ye hither;
Meal and now it mix together
Add a little oil to either;
Give the tapers here their light;
Ring the saint's bell, to affright
Far from hence the evil sprite.

For extra protection, crush a bay leaf into the door and window catches, or place a whole leaf into every crack and crevice where 'ill may enter'. This rite should be repeated at every solstice and equinox, and having your own kitchen bay to hand all year round will make this task much easier, without having to go searching for fresh bay leaves.

But if it is inadvisable for urban witches to go out and about a-wort gathering, what's the point of making an effort to recognise the various different forms of plant life growing in our locality?

Because *all* flora and fauna are part of the witch's world. By watching and recognising, we are following Nature's liturgy of the seasons and even if we cannot utilise the plants for practical use, they still offer up magical signs and symbols. For instance, take that clump of early snowdrops in the local solicitor's garden. They grow at the edge of the car park, drenched daily in exhaust fumes but for me, even on a dreary, wet wintry Monday morning, they will always evoke misty mornings with the orchard and hedgerows white with these tiny flowers. Or the potted cowslips in the garden centre that bring back childhood memories of mushrooming while the dew is still on the grass.

I'm going back to Richard Mabey on this one, because flowers do have their own associations and, for the witch, their own magical correspondences. The urban plants, flowers and shrubs we encounter might often be more exotic varieties than our native flora, but the magic is there just the same. As Mabey so rightly points out, flowers are evocative of all sorts of memories of childhood holidays, walks, meetings, people and places, with a colour, a smell, a season … *"flowers have a potent collection of qualities … they are charms, in both senses of the word."* So finding even a common weed is not just an opportunity for observation and identification; it is also one of association and correspondence. It is an experience that grows in richness and complexity the more you encounter and learn about the flower.

Already we have touched briefly on two qualities that make a *real* witch: the natural ability to heal (both practically and magically) and a proficiency of interpreting the omens. A *real* witch also has the true gift of 'sight' – that is adeptness at divining (by various different methods) the future and all it holds, from signs, dreams and visions. The *real* witch can summon the spirits of his/her ancestors (or what we may look upon as our 'guardians'), and have the skill to call upon those entities that inhabit the 'between worlds' to do his/her bidding. A *real* witch can and will curse, but rarely does, simply because of the sustained effort required to carry a successful curse through to its logical conclusion. Finally, a *real* witch must be able to find his/her way through the maze encountered during a transformational experience that all within Craft must face and, should it be necessary, to descend into Otherworld to accompany the dead on their final journey.

On too many occasions, however, a genuine urban witch will find it almost impossible to simply 'be' any of these things, because of the overspill of outside social, emotional and mental conditions that permanently invade our daily lives. On the surface, society still has all the ingredients for making life more comfortable and serene, but under the thin veneer of plenty, there is a smouldering minefield of stress and anxiety-inducing pressures. In fact, the psychic pressures on an urban witch far outweigh those of her country cousin because whereas in the country it is always possible to find a quiet corner, in the town there is that continuous tidal wave of negative psychic inter-ference (albeit unintentional) from neighbours and our immediate surroundings. This why the urban witch needs to be much *more* magically proficient when Circle working, and why it is so essential to create a special bolt-hole for meditational purposes.

Although many pagans would probably have conniptions at this suggestion, one of the most effective places for peace and meditation for the urban witch, is often a local church, especially if its foundations are very old. Remember that many were built on existing pagan sites and that nearly every village had its church dating from Saxon or Norman times – and those villages were eventually swallowed up by later urban development.

Being Welsh, I have a great love of what we call 'the voice' and will never miss an opportunity to attend choral evensong, especially if I'm anywhere near one of the great cathedrals. This isn't just a love of music, it's the peace and tranquillity – the best antidote for the pace and noise of modern living. Be conscious of the beauty and history of the building and not the division between beliefs. Go on … try it!

Chapter Three – Wildlife on your Doorstep

Craft, then, is all about inter-acting with Nature on both the spiritual and temporal levels. This means a strong awareness of the potency of the natural tides and energies that power the universe and our daily lives. The use of magic within Craft is the ability to produce results by compelling the aid of 'spirits', or by using the forces of Nature (the energy residing in both animate and inanimate objects), to empower and control the witch's imagination or Will. To become aware of these energies requires the witch to take a deeper interest in what is generally referred to as 'natural history' and be able to identify both the plants and wildlife that are part of his or her environment.

Nevertheless, it's quite amazing how many calling themselves witches have no basic knowledge of the different trees and the folk-lore surrounding them, or the behavioural patterns of the creatures they claim as their 'totem' animals! The usual excuse is that they do not have access to trees and animals because they live in a town or inner city. It is, of course, understandable that people harbour the belief that wildlife is deterred from coming into the cities and towns by the roads, noise and pollution. For many species like the red kite that was sighted in Hackney in East London, or the fastest creature on earth – the peregrine falcon that has colonised many of the major towns and cities where there is a healthy pigeon population, access is rarely a problem. Birds (including swifts and house martins), insects and bats (most of Britain's 15 species) take the aerial route, while mammals can travel freely along the land corridors of motorway verges, railway embankments and canals, which give free and easy passage. As a result, they pass unnoticed into the very heart of inner-city developments and post-industrial wastelands.

In fact, recent environmental studies have shown that more and more wildlife is being seen on a regular basis in the towns.

English Nature even goes so far as to say that many towns are better places for wildlife than the surrounding countryside. One reason is most urban areas are generously endowed with chemical-free parks and brown-field areas that have long fallen into disuse, and which are now swarming with insects and plants. Huge improvements in urban water quality are also important, with rivers that were once little better than industrial sewers - "Think of the pollution nightmare that used to be Merthyr Tydfil – now teeming with fish ... and the Tees and Tyne now important salmon rivers."

Thirty years ago, otters were one of our most threatened species, but cleaner urban water means they are now regularly seen in some of our most industrial towns and cities. The absence of mink from urban areas means that Birmingham and Middlesborough have more water voles than the surrounding countryside, while a stretch of former canal in Swindon also provides a safe haven for our little childhood friend from *Wind in the Willows*.

Added to this, suburban gardens, blossoming in the wake of the popular televised garden make-overs, now offer an improved habitat in the way of a wide variety of flowers, trees, shrubs and ponds. This has resulted in an explosion of insect life, which in turn, has attracted large numbers of birds and mammals. The attraction is supplemented by the generous provision of bird tables and nest boxes, while other species turn to plentiful (and temptingly) filled bin bags and discarded fast food containers. Urban compost heaps and frog-rich garden ponds are perfect for the harmless grass snake (especially in the centre of Swindon!). The natural food-chain is fast – and furious!

First of all, let's deal with the question of 'totem animals' for the urban witch. I have never seen the logic of magically identifying with a creature that we cannot expect to meet in a real-life close encounter. After all, we are hardly likely to meet a wolf, polar bear or tiger in Chigwell High Street. There is a resident population of bottle-nosed dolphins in the Moray Firth, members of which have been spotted near Aberdeen, St Andrews and the Firth of Forth. But if we are seeking to empower ourselves for magical work, waiting for the rare sighting of a whale or dolphin in the upper reaches of the Thames estuary, could cause the moment to be lost! *Carpe diem!* Seize the moment!

All animals and birds, and even reptiles and insects, can act as omen bearers. Traditionally, a dog/fox calling, an owl/hawk screeching, or a frog/toad croaking at the end of a ritual, tells the witch that her appeal has been successful, and that the spell has gone home. And, believe it or not, *all* of these are creatures can appear on a regular basis to the town-dweller.

Most witches see frogs as a good omen and only recently, when we were contemplating yet another move, a tiny frog marched across the sitting room floor of our urban cottage towards the hearth, where there was a blazing fire. We took this to be a positive sign for our future plans and the frog was taken outside to the log pile, before it could be accidentally stepped on or incinerated. Where on earth the creature had come from, or how it had got into the house on that cold, winter night we had no idea but there is was, as large as life in the middle of the carpet.

In some places, however, a frog entering a house was a serious indication of 'death or some equally dreadful event, as toads are known to enter human dwellings but frogs rarely do'. Frogs were widely used in cures for human ailments and it was considered unlucky to injure or kill one. Frogs and toads were often regarded as interchangeable in many localised traditions but where toads were associated with witches, frogs were viewed in a more friendly light. Toads crop up repeatedly as both ingredients and as familiars in witch-lore, and 'toad-men' were highly respected for their skills with horses, especially in East Anglia. And as I pointed out in *A Witch's Treasury of the Countryside*, toads were often kept in cottage pantries and greenhouses to keep them clear of troublesome insects.

Urban foxes (also not to be confused with *their* country cousins) are so numerous that they are now considered to be a pest in some inner cities. For many years we were visited regularly by an old dog fox, who used to lie up under the shed at night – the unmistakeable pong always alerted us to the fact that he'd been around. And it was a regular early morning occurrence when out walking the dog, to meet up with a local vixen, who crossed the park on her way for a daily offering of buttered toast from one of the elderly bungalow owners.

Foxes, like all nocturnal creatures, have been identified at some time with witchcraft and in some regions it was believed that a witch could shapeshift into a fox, but there is surprisingly little folk-lore involving the animal. Most of the fox's associations are strongly linked to the hunting tradition of the countryside, the energies of which are totally inappropriate in the town. Nevertheless, in urban areas during the peak mating season in January (when foxes are at their most vocal), the eerie barking and screaming carry long distances, particularly on cold nights.

Raptors (or birds of prey) are sighted more and more frequently in urban areas and only recently when out walking one morning, I witnessed a sparrow hawk take a collared dove from a tree outside a block of flats. It only took the blink of an eye and all that was left were a few feathers drifting down from the winter branches of the silver birch like a scene from *Watership Down*. On another occasion, a kestrel that had been perching in an old lime tree, swooped low over my head, hovered for a moment and then flew off into the bank of trees on the far side of the park.

Owls have always been associated with death, sorcery and Otherworldly affairs, so it is not surprising to find that they were believed to accompany witches on their broomstick flights. The birds were generally disliked and feared, and their screech was seen as a proverbial death-omen. In the Fens they were thought to be witches in disguise and were, if possible, shot on sight. Owls, too, can be heard (if not seen) in urban areas. Other birds of prey, however, perhaps because of their more 'noble' associations appear to be completely devoid of any native folk-lore or superstition, and (apart from the peregrine falcon) are rarely seen in towns.

These are the native fauna normally associated with traditional Craft but what is the problem in linking psychically with a robin, or a magpie, that may be a regular visitor to our garden? Robins are one of the most ferocious of birds and aggressively territorial, but they have also inspired a large amount of popular literature and folk-lore. In common with other members of the crow family, magpies have always attracted devilish significance, but they were respected by the ancient British tribes for giving out their chattering warning when wolves were about. In fact, magpies have been used as divinatory birds for hundreds of years, with the earliest known reference dating from 1159.

Exercise:
If you have, or if you can, develop an empathy with wild creatures, then you will quickly learn how to read the essential clues about how they can act as oracles in your daily life. For example: if you have a burning question or problem that needs resolving, tell yourself that the next 'sign' you see will provide the answer. As with all divinatory methods, to get the answer all we need to do is ask.

One of the most remarkable divinatory 'tools' at the urban witch's disposal, for example, is the spectacular roosting flight of starlings that takes place every evening in both town and country. In the inner cities, huge flocks of more than a million birds can be seen wheeling around and darkening the sky at dusk. Known as a 'murmuration', these impressive flighting patterns can produce the most amazing images in the sky, which are held for a second and then disperse and regroup into something else. Richard Mabey recalls their spectacular dusk flights "that have more than once nearly had me run over" while watching the birds "fold like a black cloak around the tops of the buildings round Trafalgar Square in London."

The old Welsh name means 'bird of the snow' because the starling was once a winter visitor to these shores, and would have told our ancestors that the weather was about to deteriorate. While an old Irish remedy (an ounce of starling dung, mixed with alum and white vitriol, i.e. zinc sulphates) was believed to cure afflictions ranging from ringworm to herpes! Ask your question of the starlings and see what images they produce in the sky in response.

Charm for Banishing Rats

Although they bring about fear and loathing in everyone, in our towns we all live within five feet from a rat! The now rare black rat (the old English rat) was introduced to these islands during the 11-12th centuries following excursions on the Crusades, and is infamous for carrying the fleas that transmit bubonic plague. The more common brown rat only arrived some 250 years ago, but according to superstition, rats respond well to civility and a time-honoured method of getting rid of them is to ask them politely to leave – either verbally, or written on a piece of paper that is put down their hole or pinned up nearby. A tried and tested charm is as follows:

R.A.T.S
A.R.S.T
T.S.R.A
S.T.A.R

Remember, however, that the animals have to move somewhere and if your neighbours become infested, they will probably call in the pest control man for the final solution. Rats are highly intelligent and adaptable creatures, and will probably survive Armageddon – but as a character in one of Graham Greene's novels observes: "Let's hope they never invent the wheel!" In other words, rats are an integral part of the urban witch's life and deserve our grudging respect, even if we don't want them to stay for dinner.

It would be counter-productive to list all the flora and fauna that we are likely to encounter in our different urban environments throughout the British Isles, but provided we fully understand that once we 'invite' them into our consciousness, our lives *will* invariably change. When we encounter a wild creature, we experience a sudden rush of freedom and primal instinct. Depending on the type of flora/fauna, and the way we identify with it, we can be seized by a sudden feeling of alarm or anxiety. On the other hand, discovering a common horsetail can give a sensation of timelessness, since this plant is the last surviving member of a species that flourished in the Carboniferous period, something like 300 million years ago. Not surprising that Culpeper attributed this plant to Saturn!

Our native wildlife has had a tremendous influence on customs, traditions and folk-lore. As *Fauna Britannica* points out, it is a testament to the ways in which our native animals have enriched our culture. They have provided differing local and national traditions; as well as influencing place names. They have been the inspiration for artists, composers and writers, not to mention being adopted as symbols on everything from heraldic emblems to pub signs, and commercial advertising campaigns. And last, but certainly not least for the witch's purpose, they have bequeathed the colourful superstitions, myths and legends that have enriched British folk-lore for centuries. The line between man and animal is easily crossed, and so is the line between animals and the spirit world – deity may be seen in an animal that shares some quality with him/her/it. In magic, an animal is used for its own inherent occult correspondences or associations, or because of its known link with supernatural forces.

Exercise:

To draw your 'totem' animal to you, it *will* be necessary to go outside and take time to 'stand and stare'. If you are fortunate enough to have a garden, spend the time sitting quietly with a coffee and observe. If you use the local park, or walk to work, keep your eyes open for uncharacteristic behaviour in any local fauna you encounter.

- Which creature appears to you on a fairly regular basis?

- Does one particular creature demonstrate some unexpected interest in you?

- Has a wild creature taken to regularly appearing on your 'patch'?

- Has a bird uttered a warning cry/display that prevented you from having an accident, or making a mistake?

Quite often the result is not we expect it to be in terms of a dazzling or 'all guns blazing' manifestation, and usually its appearance doesn't conform to any preconceptions we may have of our 'totem' animal.

NB: 'Totem' animal is a shamanistic term that has entered into the British pagan lexicon and is used here because it is a familiar word to all. It is not a term the author would use herself.

Also be aware that no matter what the books may say, there are no hard and fast rules governing the attributes of animals and their 'doings', since what is considered an auspicious omen in one part of the country can be a harbinger of ill-fortune in another. Even family members can differ over the same super-stition: for a friend of mine, a bird coming into the house tells of news about to arrive from afar; but for her mother it's an omen of death. Magical correspondences and associations differ from individual to individual, and the only way to recognise your own 'messenger' is to study the wildlife on your doorstep.

Chapter Four – The Urban 'Shadow World'

The urban witch has been around for a long time. The day before the coronation of Richard I in 1189, a proclamation had been made forbidding the attendance of witches at the ceremony at Westminster, although no official reason for the ban appears to have been recorded. Nevertheless, the presences of witches in London must have been a fairly common occurrence if a royal proclamation had to be issued to keep them away on that specific day. In his definitive book on witchcraft and the social order [*Witches & Neighbours*], Robin Briggs, demonstrates the ways in which beliefs about witchcraft responded to changes in pre-industrial society, as people moved from the villages to the towns looking for work and prosperity. Many of these would have been the midwives, whose skills would have been much in demand: a skill that was still the province of the 'wise women' rather than the emerging medical profession.

In *The Sociology of Health & Healing*, Professor Margaret Stacey researching Tudor and Stuart medicine and health care, tells us that given the wide range of beliefs and practices of the period, the selection of treatment was much more varied in the towns than in the countryside. Country people had to rely on folk-healers, although there were barber surgeons in a number of villages; there was much more of a choice in the towns, especially for those who could afford to pay more. Fees varied and payment in kind was possible; some practitioners treated some cases free, and even the less well off were prepared to pay if they though the treatment worthwhile. While only the upper classes could afford the elite physicians, it appears that they weren't above consulting the cunning folk and various other healers if the situation warranted it.

One of the most detailed records of the part played by urban witches comes from the famous *Chambre Ardente* Affair, probably the only witch-trial based on some element of truth. The investigation was set up by Louis XIV to examine widespread poisoning among the French nobility, with charges levelled against the greatest lords and ladies in France. Police enquiries revealed the involvement of a *devineresse* (fortune teller) named Marie Boss and an accomplice, La Dame Vigoreux, who were alleged to have supplied all manner of poisons (*poudres de succession*), in order for their clients to do away with inconvenient spouses and rivals.

Another fortune teller was implicated, the celebrated Catherine Deshayes, Widow Montvoisin, commonly known as La Voisin, who protested that her trade was merely that of chiromancy (palmistry) and physiognomy (divination by study of the face). Up to this point, however, according to *The Dictionary of Witchcraft & Demonology*, witchcraft had not been brought into the equation. "Sorcery, yes – the fortune tellers sold love philtres (*poudres pour l'amour*) and mixed their arsenic, sulphur, and vitriol with dried bats and toads, semen and menstrual blood. Nor did witchcraft figure in the evidence collected later from other fortune tellers ... Ensuing legislation banned fortune tellers, controlled the sale of poisons, and declared witchcraft a superstition ..."

The point made in citing Richard I's proclamation, Stacey's research and the *Chambre Ardent* Affair is to demonstrate that what we today would describe as witches or wise women, were obviously plentiful and highly accessible in 12th and 16th century London and 17th century Paris. Pushing aside the suspect judicial system and salacious aspect of the latter, it also establishes the fact that French nobility made regular use of these wise women's services for the purpose of divination, philtres and abortion. As time marched on, across Europe the urban sprawl crept out into the surrounding countryside, so these accomplished wise women gravitated towards the towns. Towns and cities became more densely populated and in order to earn a living, the forerunners of the 'new age' outlets were born, since there was always someone wanting to know about the future, attracting a lover, or acquiring an increase in wealth.

That patron saint of pagan wort-lore, Thomas Culpeper (himself the son of a clergyman) catered for the superstition that still surrounded healing in the 17th century. Although he was also knowledgeable about anatomy, pædiatrics and *material medica*, he was a thorn in the flesh of the august Royal College of Physicians, who considered him to be a 'vituperative quack' who practised medicine illegitimately. An integral part of Culpeper's medicine was the use of astrology, which he used throughout his work, in diagnosis, prognosis and prescription.

These historical cameos demonstrate that throughout history, what we may see as 'cunning folk' [the term used in its widest possible context] have been just as much – if not more – an accepted part of urban society than their country cousins. People from minority groups, however, can still be extremely vulnerable if they find themselves on the receiving end of their neighbours' prejudice or animosity.

Only three cottages down from where we live, a middle-aged pagan couple regularly have dog mess and other substances hurled at their window. The window and glass over the front door are festooned with pentagrams and other occult symbols, and this obviously attracts the local yobbos like a magnet, but whether through fear or prejudice, or merely 'let's wind up the witches', who can say. In congested towns and cities those neighbours who are perceived as being different, can be swiftly singled out to be the butt of someone else's ridicule or malice.

In the late 1980s and early 1990s the embryonic pagan community ran headlong into an evangelical onslaught of pagan-bashing that spread to the highest levels of the Establishment. For five years the public dined out on the salacious reporting of the national press, fuelled by accusations from social services, evangelical bodies and government officials who were all eager to climb on the media bandwagon. Finally, common sense prevailed when the so-called 'overwhelming evidence' for all these social misdemeanours was found to be non-existent.

The conflagration had started in Leeds and quickly spread to Rochdale and Nottingham, where neighbours informed on neighbours, and teachers reported children's conversations to the appropriate authorities. Anyone displaying any suggestion of new-age belief was targeted in a way that was reminiscent of the instances discussed by Robin Briggs in *Witches & Neighbours*, with crowds standing outside the victims' homes, literally baying for blood. Ironically, an earlier 1960s anti-occult campaign was rooted very firmly in rural England, and although there were discussions at parliamentary level, it quickly floundered, and there were relatively few casualties among pagan folk.

There is nothing wrong, of course, in wanting to 'come out' and make a statement about our beliefs but sometimes discretion *is* the better part of valour, particularly for the town or city-based witch. After all, anyone from *any* denomination, faith or creed who goes OTT in flamboyantly displaying symbols of their religion is automatically labelled a crank, so why should it be different for pagans? Personally, I have never owned a pentagram or any other piece of identifiably 'pagan' jewellery – yet that which I do wear is consecrated and symbolic *to me alone*. There is nothing in our home that screams 'WITCH' to the casual visitor, but the symbolism is there in every room if they only knew *how* to look.

Even if we think we're being subtle, this is not always the case. There was the story going around some years ago about the town witch who grew a tall hedge around three-sides of her garden to conceal her 'doings' from the neighbours' prying eyes. Unfortunately, the reflection of her bonfire in the glass patio doors gave the impression that the house was on fire and a neighbour called the fire brigade. The result was an embarrassed and naked witch confronting a crew of curious, lusty firemen – and it wasn't even a Beltaine rite!

As we have already discussed, interfering neighbours aside, the urban witch has a much greater problem to dealt with: the blanket malaise that often smothers many of our urban environments. This can be best likened to a good, old-fashioned smog that used to permeate everything in the inner cities. The pollution might be gone but there is a different kind of social 'smog' invading our personal space that can have a debilitating effect on a witch's life.

When we lived in the Midlands, the area was considered 'depressed' because of the long-term loss of industry, and the large number of adult males from *two* generations who were unable to find work. The people were friendly and good natured but there was an underlying lack of hope that prevented them from thinking past the next month, or having any ambition for their children, or grandchildren. In moving to East Anglia, a different type of malaise was caused by the transient population failing to establish any community roots, and exacerbated by a serious drink-drugs problem amongst the workers that spilled out onto the streets at night.

Even if our own particular 'patch' is peaceful enough, each time we go shopping or travel to work, the evidence of mindless vandalism and barely suppressed aggression confronts us on all sides. Broken bottles and discarded beer cans litter the streets; the remains of a previous night's take-away deposited by the bus stop. Chewing gum, vomit and spittle make walking a hazard. Plants ripped from the municipal beds, hurled about in a frenzied nocturnal flower battle and trampled under foot. In parks and gardens there are swaths of daffodils beheaded, or stolen by someone looking for a cheap bouquet. The constant noise of bawling children accompanied by yelling disgruntled mothers. The 24-7 smell of fast food, and the intrusive sound of passing car stereos, played at full blast ...

Undeniably, this kind of environment is not conducive to successful magical working, because of the constant barrage of negative energy a witch confronts at every turn. Unfortunately, we cannot always choose where we want to live but we can *learn to live how we choose,* and to block out the things that can be psychically (and spiritually) damaging to our functioning on a magical and spiritual level.

In Chapter Two we discussed some simple steps to protect our home in order to create a safe haven for magical working, but each time we come back into our house or flat, we bring in negative energy every time we open the door. What we now need to do, is to examine ways of protecting ourselves from all the negative vibes we encounter during our daily routine. We need to wrap ourselves in a protective bubble, so that the flotsam and jetsam of daily living becomes like water off the proverbial duck's back!

In other words, we need to empower *ourselves* psychically to withstand the outside pressures that threaten our inner calm. As I've said before, I've had countless conversations with pagans who believe themselves to be the victim of a psychic attack because they feel prey to a permanent mental, physical and emotional drain. In a way they are correct, but the 'attack' is the result of magical arrogance or ignorance, rather than anything directed at them from some known or unknown enemy.

Without delving into the dominion of ritual magic, there are numerous parasitic entities that inhabit the inner and outer astral realms, which feed off the negative impulses generated by thousands of people confined within a less than perfect environment. They have been described as strange, parasitic creatures, lost souls seeking to stretch across the abyss and make contact with the warm, constant flow of humanity. Like all parasites, these astral shells prefer to feed off a healthy host than an enfeebled one, and the unwary witchlet who has insufficient magical protection *will* attract such entities like a beacon, especially when they begin to generate psychic energy during early ritual workings. To withstand this unwanted psychic barrage, the urban witch needs to be protected at *all* times, and not just when working in Circle.

The Witch's Pouch and power objects

One of the most effective methods of protection is the acquisition of the magical pouch, containing a selection of 'power objects' that are yours, and yours alone. The pouch should *never* be touched or opened by anyone else, otherwise the potency of the contents will be dispersed – much like the legend of Pandora's box. This is a universal and age-old shamanic concept but one that is equally as valuable in the 21st century.

The pouch can be made from any material but it is good idea to choose one of a fairly durable nature – if you find something suitable ready-made, this is fine. Ideally, as the pouch should always be with you in a pocket, bag or briefcase, don't go for anything too cumbersome because I have seen them the size of the Hollywood bag of jewels so beloved by Robin Hood movie-makers, and it doesn't make them any more potent!

The pouch itself should be ritually cleansed and consecrated *but the items that go in it should not.* This is because you are selecting items that carry a 'buzz' of their own, and all you will do is destroy the natural propensities that accompany each find. Remember that herbs and plants will quickly dry and turn to dust, and the elegant magpie's feather will all too soon become tatty. Choose more enduring items – like the friend who carries a piece of coal in her pouch … it was once a little carved figure but the constant battering inside the pouch has rendered it unrecognisable. Nevertheless for her it still remains a serious power object.

Without giving any secrets away, one object I carry in my own pouch is an old-fashioned, coloured glass marble. I discovered this buried deep in the roots of a tree felled in the winter gales.

The mangled roots looked like the head of a dragon and, glinting in the sunlight, was the 'eye' – a marble lost there by some long-departed child. To anyone else it would merely be a coloured marble, but it has been a power object of mine for many years because of the circumstances surrounding its find.

Don't be in any rush to acquire these items. Discovery can be quite by accident. Sitting on a park bench I discovered a hagstone in the gravel at my feet ... how many other people had stepped over, on and by such a precious object? Another 'find' was a silver charm for my 'totem animal' on a bric-a-brac stall at a local church bazaar. Don't go searching, just learn to keep your eyes open for such treasures but do avoid the expensive polished crystals from the high street shop or pagan fair – a piece of home-growth quartz or pebble can pack just as good a punch.

Once assembled, our pouch is our own magical power-pack or psychic generator, that can be used to channel healing or protective energy, even if we are away from our home environment. It can be recharged now and again by taking it into Circle, and it will transmit a powerful aura to protect against all the negative vibrations discussed earlier in this Chapter.

Talismans and amulets

The difference between an amulet and a talisman as a magical tool lies in the preparation rather than the purpose. Both are extremely ancient forms of magical protection and highly potent tools of power, but we need to understand when and how to use them. Most people (if they're honest) will admit to having a lucky 'piece' that they carry around ... and very few of them are pagan. The superstition surrounding amulets goes back to ancient Egypt and it's still going strong!

Preparation of the amulet

An amulet is with us at all times, often in the form of a piece of jewellery: i.e. a ring, key fob, pendant or just carried loose in a bag or pocket. It is worn to deflect trouble and adversity in a very general sense. In other words, a good luck charm to turn away negative influences.

An amulet requires little or no preparation, particularly if it is something given to us in friendship – like a hagstone, or significant silver coin, for example. Once we have recognised or accepted its 'lucky' or protective powers, it should never be touched by anyone else; unless we choose to give it away as a gesture of friendship.

Amulets can be, or made of almost anything, so long as it has some magic significance for *you*. Remember that a witch never has to explain her/himself to anyone, not even another witch, and what you choose (or whatever chooses you) in terms of magical objects, is between you and *your own* integrity as a witch.

Preparation of the talisman

A talisman is only carried for a limited period while the spell is activated, and is aimed at a specific purpose or outcome. The material it is made from depends on the nature of the ritual used to empower it and it requires a lengthy operation to set all this magical brouhaha in motion. The exact nature of the talisman's protective power will be governed by the amount of effort and concentration that goes into the final preparation.

An ideal material for creating a talisman is heavy-duty silver baking foil, marked out with a blunt pencil so that the engraving can be clearly read. Because of the complexity of the preparation, a witch should have a working knowledge of magical correspondences and, if possible, access to magical scripts – particularly the Theban alphabet, which is often used for talismanic inscriptions. However, as David Conway points out in *The Complete Magic Primer*, many of the authors of magical books are not as erudite as they might like you to think. When we begin to study magical books it quickly becomes apparent that much of what we read is blatant gobbledegook – simply because magical practitioners have always had a liking for making things as complicated as possible and "what may look at first like Greek or Hebrew often consists only of English words transcribed into Greek or Hebrew characters."

So let's keep it simple to begin with, and stick to making a talisman for protection against ... say ... burglary if this is prevalent where you live. Now if we're talking about protection and/or retribution here, we're not looking for a dose of warts for anyone taking your property! Think cosmic watch-dog ... Cerebus, guardian of the Gates of Hades ... in British folk-lore we have the Gabriel Hounds, or Hounds of Hell *('summoned by a witch's spell')* ... think like a witch ... think dangerous.

Take a circle of heavy, silver baking foil and a blunt pencil. If your drawing skills aren't up to scratch, use Words of Power and engrave your protector's name around the outer rim of the circle. In other words, you are unleashing the wrath of the protector against anyone who dares to enter your home uninvited, and you are ultimately demanding physical evidence that revenge has been extracted by chanting:

> *When once the sin has fully acted been,*
> *Then is the horror of the trespass seen*

Place the talisman at the point in the house where you perceive the weakness in your defences, i.e. a vulnerable window or door. Slide it under the threshold, or between the timbers of the frame and leave it in place. Unfortunately, we live in a hazardous society and as witches, we are merely protecting ourselves, our family and our homes from violation. This is where the morality of 'And it harm none ...' is called into question.

It is also perhaps becoming clear why *Traditional Witchcraft for Urban Living* doesn't begin with the usual claptrap about acquiring the right magical equipment and how to celebrate the Wheel of the Year. The urban witch has more important things to learn, and first and foremost is understanding both the blessings *and* the dangers associated with our environment *before* the dressing up stage is reached!

Chapter Five – Observance and Celebration

Hopefully, now that we've got the unique problems of urban witchcraft into some sort of perspective, let's consider how we can bring ritual observance into practice. Many of the old seasonal observations were absorbed into the Christian religion and most traditional witches still refer to them by the names of the Church calendar, rather than the Celtic versions that were reconstituted in the early 1980s. Many of the customs that survive to the present day, have their origins in these pre-Christian seasonal festivals, with those around Yule and Easter surviving almost intact.

All events in the old pagan year have their roots in the agricultural calendar, which is usually a completely alien concept to the town-dweller. After all, what empathy does the city-born pagan have with tripping around the fields gathering flowers and produce in the spring and summer, or symbolically scattering ashes and wheat in the autumn and winter? How can these unfamiliar customs float the spiritual boat of an urban witch? And how can we focus our magical energy on festivals for which we have no real understanding?

It would, however, be a sad old world if we didn't find some joy in our beliefs and most of those old pagan festivals were joyous times. In *A Witch's Treasury for Hearth & Garden*, the author suggested many ways in which we can celebrate the seasons by throwing our homes open for some normal, everyday enter-taining, with non-pagan guests not even being aware of what they are helping us to celebrate. Half the fun is researching the background of the Old Ways and adapting them to suit our contemporary urban life-style.

Twelfth Night: 6th January

There are lots of superstitions surrounding Twelfth Night but this is when traditional witches often celebrate Old Yule (according to the Julian Calendar), while non-pagans will be taking down the festive decorations to avoid ill-luck in the coming year. This is also the time to toast the fruit trees to ensure a bumper harvest according to this 17th century rhyme.

> *Wassail the trees, that they may bear*
> *You many a plum and many a pear;*
> *For more or less fruits they will bring*
> *As you do give them wassailing.*

In *The Witch's Treasury of the Countryside*, I pointed out that after the introduction of the Gregorian calendar, Twelfth Night was often celebrated with far more feasting and merrymaking than Christmas, the former being observed as a religious ceremony. Because of the traditional connections with the Lord of Misrule, an ideal celebration would be a fancy dress party with lots of winter food on the buffet table, mulled wine and good quality cider. In some parts of the country bonfires were customary, so lots of candles or a patio fire would be appropriate.

Candlemas (Imbolc) 2nd February

Traditionally Imbolc was the festival to mark the start of the Celtic lambing season but in the 5th century this was changed to Candlemas in the Church calendar. The only lamb we see will probably be roasted and served with mint sauce, but this 17th century rhyme by Robert Herrick gives us an insight into customs that were resurrected, having been kept under wraps during the dark days of the Commonwealth (1649-1660).

Ceremonies for Candlemas Day

> *Kindle the Christmas brand, and then*
> *Till sunset let it burn,*

Which quenched, then lay it up again
Till Christmas next return.

Part must be kept, wherewith to teend
The Christmas log next year,
And where 'tis safely kept, the fiend
Can do no mischief here

This can be a celebration of new beginnings and your guests don't necessarily have to be of pagan persuasion to enjoy it. *The Witch's Treasury of Hearth & Garden* suggests that this is a time for sharing and promise for the future – and an ideal time for a ritual gesture of friendship with a large casserole to represent the Caldron of Plenty, together with the sharing of bread and salt, eaten by candle-light.

Spring or Vernal Equinox: 21st March

Magically, the tides around this time are extremely strong and it takes a brave witch to stick her head over the parapet and harness the energies that accompany *this* annual event. The Vernal Equinox is part of the yearly sun-cycle and strongly influenced by masculine energy. In modern times, the observation has been relegated to being classed as a 'minor sabbat' but personally I would find this time much more magically stimulating than the highly suspect calendar date of Beltaine. I think this extract from one of Ben Johnson's masques [1572-1637] would be highly appropriate for any Circle working at this time.

Pan's Anniversary (or The Shepherd's Holiday)

Thus begin the yearly rites
Are due to Pan on these bright nights;
His morn now rises and invites
To sports, to dances and delights:

All envious and profane, away;
This is the shepherd's holiday

This is a very good time to work positively for growth and future plans; for new life and fresh beginnings. The precession of the equinoxes (not to mention the alterations to the civil calendars) has drastically altered the alignment between the natural cycle and the modern calendar dates of these old festivals. Logic tells us that the solstices and equinoxes would have governed the lives of our ancestors and so the Vernal Equinox would have been an important time of the year; when the hours of light and dark were equal and heralded the coming of spring. Most cultures reflect this time with some form of flower or sowing festival.

Easter (Ostara)

Easter is the only moveable feast in the Church calendar, which falls according to the old pagan lunar cycle ... on the first Sunday following the first full moon after the Spring Equinox. This is a traditional festival in honour of the Anglo-Saxon goddess of spring, Eostre, whose symbol is our native brown hare. Like all pagan spring festivals, there is always an element of flirtation and fun, as is reflected in this 17th century charm with its *double entendre*.

A Charm

This I'll tell ye by the way,
Maidens, when ye leavens lay,
Cross your dough, and your despatch
Will be better for your batch

Easter celebrations can be organised to include those from every age group in searching out the Easter bunny (chocolate rabbits) and an Easter egg hunt. Lots of fruit bread and hot-cross buns with lots of spices will compensate if the day is cold and wet. All the traditional customs that take place at this time have a community spirit, so use your imagination and get friends involved.

Roodmas (Beltaine) 31st April

Beltaine was celebrated with the lighting of the Bel-fire in honour of the sun god and heralded the start of a raunchy festival of love-making and feasting. It is a time of 'coming together' – no pun intended! – when couples can work magically together for a year of health, wealth and prosperity. In *British Folk Customs* there are several pages of the different ways in which May is celebrated through the British Isles and there is sure to be a localised custom in your area. Everyone knows the superstition of washing your face in the dew on May morning for a good complexion all year and to bring luck – here is a slight variation that dates back to the 17th century.

A Charm

In the morning when ye rise
Wash your hands and cleanse your eyes;
Next, be sure you have a care
To disperse the water far,
For as far as that doth light
So far keeps the evil sprite.

Garlands of flowers and green leaves are part of the May celebrations, as is the maypole, an ancient fertility emblem belonging to the beginning of summer. A miniature version can be garlanded with flowers and ribbons and given to couples who could benefit from some Beltaine good-wishing! A good way to celebrate the festival would be to compile a guest list made up of couples and entertain them at home, or arrange for a group of you to go out for the evening somewhere romantic.

Mid Summer or Summer Solstice : 21st June

The longest day of the year and known as Midsummer until the Church calendar moved the day to the 24th to coincide with the feast of St John. In pre-Christian times, bonfires were lit to give aid to the sun, who was now at his peak and beginning to wane. Midsummer fires were known all over Europe and people danced around them on the hills or on village greens. It was also the custom for young men to leap through the flames and drive cattle through the dying embers

The Dance

Round-a, round-a, keep your ring:
To the glorious sun we sing –
He that wears the flaming rays,
And th' imperial crown of bays,
Him with shouts and songs we praise.

This is the perfect time for a magical rite of purification as the sun rises or sets on this, the longest day of the year. In ancient times it was a fire-festival of great importance and one that the urban witch would be wise to observe. The above is a 'round dance' that witches use to imitate the movement of the cosmos and the seasons. It is a dance of homage and intended to raise the cone of power, and often has a hypnotic effect if performed correctly. These dances united the witch with nature and summoned power for spells and invocations. Celebrate with a modest garden-party for family and friends. Use the leaves from your kitchen bay to flavour the food, or use as decoration.

Lammas (Lughnasad) 1st August

Traditionally the celebration of the first cutting of the harvest and an offering of bread made from the first corn. Although the harvest is the most important time of the year for the country witch, we in the towns have very little to do with this essentially rural custom. We shop in supermarkets and probably give very little thought to where our food comes from, never mind whether it's traditionally in season or not. Thankfully, this attitude is beginning to change and people are beginning to take a vested interest in what they eat, with Farmers' Markets now thriving in towns and cities.

Harvest Time

The boughs do shake and bells do ring,
So merrily comes our harvest in,
Our harvest in, our harvest in,
So merrily comes our harvest in.

We've ploughed, we've sowed,
We've reaped, we've mowed,
We've got our harvest in.

As part of the celebration, make the effort to visit your local Farmers' Market and prepare a meal to welcome the produce from the harvest into town. This first festival lacks the solemnity of the next and should therefore be a merry family occasion.

Autumn Equinox : 21st September

Perhaps one of the most magical times of the year, when day and night are equally divided and the last of the harvest has been gathered in. It is a time to complete old business as we head towards a traditional time for rest, relaxation, reflection and the slowing down of the year. This is where we can look back on something that has been worked for and celebrate the achievement of its success; perhaps the project was carried through, despite the odds against and harassments of the long months behind us. The harvest-home songs differ slightly from county to county, but perhaps the most well-known and relevant to pagan belief is ...

Sir John Barleycorn

There came three men from out of the west
Their victory to try;
And they have ta'en a solemn oath,
Poor Barleycorn should die ...

The death of Sir John Barleycorn is a popular version of the ancient death of the Corn King, which brings blessings and promises a secure future. This more masculine harvest observance is more in keeping with a wake and the Harvest Supper is still served in many rural areas. The most common relic of this old custom, however, is the Harvest Festival, which was introduced in Victorian times, and is still celebrated in parishes all over England. In more urban churches you're more likely to find cans of baked beans rather than plaited loaves and corn dollies, but the spirit of the harvest celebration lives on in our subconscious.

Hallowmas (Samhain) 31st October

All Hallows is the beginning of the dark, winter half of the year and a time for honouring the ancestors. This is a sombre occasion in the witch's year and certainly *not* a time for celebration. To use a familiar phrase, 'it is when the veil between the worlds is at its thinnest', and a candle placed at the window can help the ancestors to come home. Some traditional witches hold a 'Dumb Supper' to mark the occasion, setting an empty place at the table for any wandering spirit who cares to partake of the offerings.

And heavy is the tread
Of the living; but the dead
Returning lightly dance ...

From pre-Christian times, this darkening time of the year has been associated with ancestral ghosts, unquiet spirits and death. Ritual fires were kindled on hilltops for the purification of the people and the land but unlike the Bel-fires that were lit at dawn, the Hallow-fires were lit at dusk. Much of what we see in the towns that pass for Hallowe'en rites are imported from America, and if our 'nanny State' is so keen to impose legislation on things that denigrate a person's beliefs, I for one would vote to outlaw 'Trick or Treating'!

Midwinter Festival or Winter Solstice: 21st December

This celebration to welcome the rebirth of the Sun and renewal for the coming year also dates from pre-Christian times, and is a custom for many cultures throughout the world. It is the shortest day of the year, and from now on the days get longer. For us, it is one of the most important days of the calendar because of its ancient cross-cultural symbolism, which makes it a very magical *and* holy time indeed.

> *Our life is short, and our days are run*
> *As fast away as does the sun;*
> *And, as a vapour or a drop of rain*
> *Once lost, can ne'er be found again.*

On a personal note, we use this as the principal Yuletide feast-day for close friends who will be otherwise engaged with family commitments on Christmas Day. In other words, we push the boat out and serve the richest food and best wines to mark the occasion.

Yuletide

This is a Norse fire-festival that starts at the time of the Winter Solstice and lasts for about 12 days. The main focus is the Yule log that was renewed at the hearth every year, similar to the custom given for Candlemas. It was considered unlucky not to save a piece of the wood to light the fire at the next Yuletide celebration, while the ash from the log was kept to be sprinkled on the land to ensure the fertility of crops and livestock. This 17th century rhyme could be used as a toast, and reflects the traditional feasting aspects of the holiday rather than its spiritual ones.

Ceremonies for Christmas

Come bring with a noise,
My merry boys,
The Christmas log to the firing,
While our good dame, she
Bids ye all be free,
And drink to your hearts' desiring.

Falling at the time of Christmas in the Church calendar, it is also a celebration of rebirth and renewal, so any witch can join in any of these celebrations with a clear conscience. Most of what are seen as traditional Christmas symbols are, in fact, pagan in origin and the bringing of holly, ivy and mistletoe into the house to be garlanded with ribbons is a very old custom indeed.

As we've seen, there's no escaping the fact that the origins of nearly all of our pagan festivals *are* agriculturally-based, but there is no reason why the urban witch can't adapt the celebrations for use within the town. This dual approach has been going on for hundreds of years as the populace moved from the countryside, taking their customs with them. It just needs a bit of imagination, that's all!

Chapter Six – Magical Techniques for Confined Spaces

By now the urban witch should be more than aware (but not, we hope, paranoid) about the hazards of performing blasé and careless magical rituals, without the correct levels of protection. Hopefully, all the magical cleansing and protective preparations have been carried out so that *'all good stayeth in, and all bad keepeth out'*, ensuring that both our home and family, and ourselves are free from negative influences. Now, and only now, are we ready to …

Cast the Circle

Let's begin by defining exactly what the Circle represents and what it does. Firstly, the Circle is a symbol of 'all things' and an emblem of 'All is One', combining all the various phenomena of the universe and linking them together in Unity. The Circle represents the moon (with its quarters shaded) and the sun (a circle with a dot in the centre). While circumambulation, or moving around something in a circular manner, is a universal element of magical and religious rites from ancient times to the present day, and plays an important part in both traditional and contemporary witchcraft.

Secondly, in magical working, the Circle protects from any negative or hostile intrusion by creating a barrier between this world and Other World. It also acts as a 'holding tank' for the magical energy raised during the Circle working, which is to be harnessed and directed at the matter in hand. If it were not for the Circle, the energy would flow off in all directions and dissipate; the Circle keeps it confined to a small area and concentrates it.

The traditional Circle should be nine feet in diameter, cast by moving 'deosil' or 'sun-wise' [clockwise] and marked out by a variety of different methods according to Tradition. Under certain circumstances (and not necessary with any 'evil' intent) the Circle will be cast by moving 'widdershins', a word derived from an Anglo-Saxon phrase meaning 'to walk against', i.e. to walk against the direction of the sun (anti-clockwise).

All of this is fine, provided that we have the space in our urban stronghold to execute the prescribed ritual without having to climb over furniture, or stubbing a toe on the fireplace. In realistic terms, living in a bedsit, or utilising a standard 10x10foot furnished room, we'll never get a clear run at a nine-foot Circle!

So what are the alternatives?

What we need to have foremost in our mind is the concept of protection and containment. So let's discard that strange idea of being able to cast a mini-Circle on a table in front of us ... exactly *what* is it protecting or charging, if our hands are passing in and out of it all the time? Whatever method we choose for Circle-casting, it is imperative that the boundary is *never* broken during the working. Therefore, logic tells us, the Circle must be large enough to contain ourselves, plus any working 'tools' we need for the ritual.

How can we achieve this?

We return to the idea of the protective bubble while we perform our magical rite. We don't just cast a horizontal protection, we extend the barrier above and below, so that we are completely enclosed in a sphere of blue light. Simply sitting on the floor and visualising a shimmering ball of blue light building up around us can achieve this. Of course, there needs to be the element of psycho-drama injected into the proceedings to help build up the *power* but before we begin, it is necessary to accept that there *are* other alternatives to the conventional methods of magical scene-setting.

To all intent and purpose, when setting up the Circle we are preparing a sacred space, which requires ritual purification and consecration if the spell is to work properly. This is not always possible when living space is at a premium and one solution is to invest in one of those small Eastern prayer mats that can be bought at most markets, esoteric shops or from e-bay. Needless to say, the mat should be kept folded away at all times when not in ritual use, but it does offer a small but clearly defined area in which to work. This technique can also apply for anyone confined to a bedroom or wheelchair, where a lack of personal space creates a problem.

Before setting up any form of Circle, we align ourselves with the four cardinal points of the compass. In a large sector of esoteric belief, the North is considered to be the 'place of power' and so it makes sense to position ourselves facing that direction. In most magical workings we will be utilising or drawing upon the power of the Elements, so we must be sure we understand what each one represents. For example:

North/Earth: The colour normally associated with Earth is green (foliage), although black (soil) would also be acceptable. Traditionally represented by bowl of earth, salt or sand. Elemental Earth gives a feeling of security, symbolised by the 'mother' and the harvest.

East/Air: The colour normally associated with Air is yellow or white. Traditionally represented by burning incense (joss or cones). Elemental Air brings lightness and freedom of spirit, as well as being a universal symbol of irresistible force and uncontrollable power.

South/Fire: The colour normally associated with Fire is red or orange. Traditionally represented by a lighted candle. Elemental Fire is the symbol of warmth, passion … and danger, offering the welcome of a glowing hearth or an uncontrollable conflagration that destroys everything in its path.

West/Water: The colour normally associated with Water is blue. Traditionally represented by a bowl of *natural* water. Elemental Water is the universal symbol of primal mystery.

Before casting our Circle we must also ensure that we are pure in body and mind, either by a short meditation and/or ritual bathing. This not only a ritual cleansing, it has a practical element, too. By taking a breather and creating a moment of calm before entering a sacred space, we are switching off from the here and now, and leaving the mundane world *outside* the Circle. Create a relaxing atmosphere by playing gentle music in the background (to mask any extraneous noises) and soften the lights by placing candles at safe points around the room. If you chose to mark the quarters (or Compass) with the traditional elements, ensure nothing can be knocked over as a result of any meditational reaction, or the rite will be spoiled.

Now … roll out your prayer mat, sit down and make yourself comfortable. When you are ready, visualise a sphere of electric blue light surrounding you, above and below where you are sitting, enclosing you in its sacred bubble. It often helps to use a personal chant to raise the level of power within the Circle – this should be short and repetitive, and can be murmured softly rather than proclaimed aloud. Feel the energy build within the Circle; become familiar with the sensation and when you have finished, banish it with a word of thanks followed by visualising it being drawn in through your nostrils as a deep breath, and then expelled through the mouth. Practice this exercise a few times without thinking about using the Circle energy for any magical purpose.

Remember that every time we perform a Circle working we are tuning in to the natural energies that surround us. In *Spells,*

Charms, Talismans & Amulets, Pamela Ball makes an interesting point that we should always bear in mind that any changes that take place as a result of magical or meditational practice, initially happen on the inner planes. This change is far more subtle than whatever happens on an outer level. *"Becoming aware of what is happening on both levels will give you a much better perception of everything around you and how the various interactions take place."*

In other words, when we start messing about with different levels of consciousness we will be opening ourselves up as a receptor for all manner of psychic impulses and, as Ball continues: *"Your own consciousness will become sensitive to the subtle energies available to you and there will be more evidence that you are living in harmony with all aspects of Nature."* Now we are ready to ...

Cast the Spell

As an urban witch we've secured the safety of our home and person, battened down the security of our Circle, and now we're ready for our first spell casting ... but first a moment of reflection.

Pick up any modern book on witchcraft and they're crammed full with charms and spells to find love, money or a job. Okay ... you're done the business and met some divine bloke/bird down at the wine bar, Great-Aunt Bessie's died and left you a tidy sum, and an unexpected career move has you working six months of the year in the Bahamas ... so now what? Should we *have* to resort to magic to continually sort out our love life, finances and career prospects? And if the magic works for us, who's to say that it might be robbing someone else of *their* partner, inheritance or promotion. Magic is, and always has been, a double-edged sword, so we must be doubly careful how we wield it.

Let's start with that old magical chestnut – *the luv spell*! If it goes against someone's natural inclinations (i.e. gender bending to use a good old-fashioned term), or if the victim belongs to someone else, then *it's black magic*, however you want to glitz it up in your own mind. If you're looking for Prince(ss) Charming and expect magical impulses to deliver them to your door gift-wrapped and eager, I'd have to say get off your backside and get out more! And if you're spell-casting to make yourself more attractive to the opposite sex, try checking yourself out in the mirror before going any further.

If, on the other hand, you're sending out a call on the astral and you're convinced that you're doing everything in your power to be in the right place at the right time, do be careful what you ask for – or you might just get it! In magical working the wording must be precise or there could be some nasty shocks along the way, so take your time in drawing up a list of attributes you'd like to find in a new partner. An acquaintance generated some pretty heavy artillery in attracting her new mate, who on the surface was everything she'd asked for. Except that three months after the wedding she discovered the hard way that he'd got a violent side to his nature ... she'd forgotten to add kindness to her list!

In the current 'consumer credit crisis' everyone is feeling the pinch, so you might be a long time waiting for a windfall, even with a bit of magical assistance thrown in. Rather than a *"Gissus the money"* type of spell-casting, go for a divinatory or medita-tional result. Another acquaintance used this method and within days spotted a feature in a national newspaper that gave her all the information she needed to sort out her financial problems. With advice and support from an outside agency she was able to clear her debts within six months, but if she'd relied solely on a 'money spell' and waited for the cash to miraculously appear in her bank account, the problem would have escalated totally out of control. Spells are influenced by the amount of effort put into them, but if you're content to just fool about with a coloured candle and 'money drawing' anointing oil on a Thursday evening, the desired results might be a long time in the coming. Use magical knowledge to open the right channels in *your mind*, and be receptive to any information, ideas or advice that comes to your attention. Magic works in mysterious ways.

Likewise in the career stakes, do be careful what you ask for and *how* you ask for it. Like the witchlet who went into a spell-casting saying she wanted to work with dogs or horses … and found herself working for the local bookmaker! Spell-casting is a very exact science and should not be undertaken in a spirit of levity, despite what the books offering 'spells and rituals to attract all the good things in life' may tell you.

It ain't that easy.

To Cast The Spell

The most beneficial outcome of any spell will depend on using the correct phase of the lunar cycle (tide) and the appropriate magical correspondences. For the beginner, there may be safety in following the instructions in a main-stream spell book but as we become more proficient, we will recognise the need to draw in *all* the power at our disposal. We must move from linear to lateral thinking, also taking into account, for example, our own current physical health and weather conditions. Our body isn't a magical generator, it's a conduit for *channelling* magical energy, and if it isn't functioning properly, then any outcome may lack the necessary punch we're expecting. Likewise, a spell for bringing calm into our lives may be disrupted by a thunder-storm, or gale-force winds outside.

All these different influences are merely 'tools' that we call upon to empower our magical workings. We can fill our working space with £££'s worth of ritual equipment but if we haven't tuned-in to the right magical or Elemental correspondences, that pretty, hand-carved, £100 wooden athame might just as well be used for kindling the Bel-fire!

The rural witch will always know when the different phases of the moon fall during any given month and, weather permitting, will be able to chart its path across the night sky. The urban witch can go from one month's end to another without even getting a glimpse of the moon. Nevertheless, it's *there*, and its natural tides are waxing and waning whether we can see it or not. Invest in a calendar, diary or newspaper that gives the relevant information on a daily basis.

Lunar Cycles:

For the first two weeks of the lunar month, from the New Moon to the Full Moon, the moon is waxing or increasing in size. This is the time to cast spells for expansion and increase ... now think laterally ... We may need to perform a working *to lessen* the influence or control that somebody or something has over us, but can't wait until the waning phase of the moon. In this instance our focus would be on building up resistance and strengthening our resolve in order to achieve our desired result. In other words, get used to looking at problems from both sides.

For example, we've all had friendships that have eventually become a nuisance. Perhaps the person concerned won't accept that we've have made changes to our own life and have moved on. They wish to remain in our 'time-warp, wine-bar days', while we've settled down in a new relationship. Or an old friend has just got a divorce and is camped out at our place, with no signs of moving out. These are situations that require subtle handling, rather than acting in anger ... focus on *setting them free from their dependency*, rather than roughly pushing them away.

- Thursday governs the area of friendship (even one we wish to end), and the spell should be cast either three hours before sunrise, or three hours after sunset.

- The magical correspondences, which are associated with Thursday (and its ruling planet, Jupiter), are a purple candle, ash and/or oak wood (shavings) and sage (dried or fresh).

- With a black pen, write on a small square of clean white paper the name of the friend, and let the ink dry. Remember the aim is to finish on a positive note, not a negative one.

- Fold the paper into an envelope to contain the shavings and herb and, using a small pair of tongs or tweezers, hold the paper in the candle flame. Make sure everything is reduced to ash. Visualise the friend moving away from you in the form of a bird being released from a cage.

- Collect the ash in a small container (or glass jar) and take them outside to an open space. Scatter the ash to the four winds saying: *Let* [Name's] *spirit be open and free; Let* [Name's] *thoughts be away from me. So mote it be.*

- Putting it somewhere safe, allow the purple candle to burn out. Do not blow it out, as this is your offering.

From the Full Moon to the Dark of the Moon, the moon is waning or shrinking in size and the time to perform workings for contraction and decrease. Here our focus would be on breaking down barriers and removing any opposition, so that our plans can go full steam ahead. Here we have to be honest with ourselves and admit that often we create our own obstacles to personal advancement, but it's easier to blame something or someone else for our failure to progress. Remember the old adage: *"You can't change anything but yourself, but in changing yourself, everything changes around you."* In other words, we must take responsibility for our actions. For example:

Unfortunately, nearly all of us go through the experience of divorce or separation at some stage in our lives, and often the process can drag on because neither side will agree to the demands of the other. What we would be looking for here is a spell for reconciliation: not for getting back together but for re-establishing communication, for removing the obstacles that are preventing us from moving on. And on reflection, how many of the problems are caused by *our own* stubbornness, pride or sheer bloody-mindedness?

- Friday governs the area of marriage and relationships (even those we wish to end), and the spell should be cast either three hours before sunrise or three hours after sunset.

- The magical correspondences, which are associated with Friday (and its ruling planet, Venus), are a light green or pink candle, sycamore wood (shavings) and rose or carnation petals (fresh or dried). Also a breast feather from a pigeon or dove.

- In green or pink ink, write the former partner's name on a small square of clean white paper. Try to banish any thoughts of anger or resentment.

- Fold the paper into an envelope to contain the shavings and petals and, using a small pair of tongs or tweezers, hold the paper in the candle flame. Make sure everything is reduced to ash. Visualise the former partner's demands in the form of a letter on one side of a set of old-fashioned scales; hold the feather in the palm of the hand and imagine it resting on the other side of the scales. Watch as the two sides of the scales begin to balance, eventually levelling out with equal weight. Say: *"I command negativity, problems, obstacles, ill-feeling and selfishness to be gone. So mote it be."* Repeat this four times to the four cardinal points of the compass.

Spell casting around the Dark of the Moon is a much more emotive subject. Some spell books ignore this phase completely, while other waffle on about anything and nothing. Whether this is to shield the beginner from wading into 'dark waters' before they're ready, or to mask the author's ignorance, I'm never sure. Most traditional witches of *my* acquaintance relish a dark moon working because of its *"Hang on to your hats, boys!"* type of magical energy. But when would we call upon it?

In an earlier chapter we discuss the making of a talisman for protection against burglary but if we're talking about retribution for an actual crime we're into a whole different ball-game altogether. As I've said before, a true witch can and *will* curse, and providing the punishment fits the crime, there is nothing wrong in drawing on any weapon in our armoury. Anyone, however, who throws curses about for a petty slight, or to get their own back for some real or imagined insult, really needs to get out more. On the other hand, any act of deliberate cruelty towards children or animals, is open season as far as I'm concerned ... and if it's personal then that adds extra *oomph* to the spell. Forget about 'and it harm none', just start as you mean to go on: *"I summon the Power that is mine by right, in order to bring about my purpose. So Mote it Be!"*

As far as a good, old-fashioned cursing is concerned, I'm going to cite a completely OTT example in the famous 'Blacksmith's Curse' from *White Horse: Equine Magical Lore* by Rupert Percy. The author recommends it be used on 'anyone harming or attempting to harm a horse', a desperately horrible practice that surfaces periodically in rural communities. There are, however, enough horror stories emanating from our towns and cities to warrant adapting the following, which can be used to bring retribution on perpetrators who are unknown, and who may be some distance away from the sender.

May their skull be crushed as the iron is crushed by the hammer.
May their bowels be torn as the iron is seized by the tongs.

May their blood spurt from their veins as the sparks fly from beneath the hammer.

May their hearts freeze from cold as the iron is cooled in water.

Grisly stuff indeed, but Dark of the Moon energies don't have to be used just for sorting out the evil folk on the planet. This is an extremely powerful energy and, if harnessed correctly, can cut a swathe through most obstacles in its path: which is why seasoned witches have a marked preference for the 'dark face of the moon'.

Equipment

Finally, we've got around to discussing magical equipment, and it must be obvious by now, that a lot of expensive paraphernalia isn't necessary for traditional Craft magic. I personally only own *two* items of ritual regalia … my knife and my cord but these are important symbolic representations pertinent to my *own Craft roots*, and not essential to the successful outcome of any magical working.

Generally speaking, the carrying of a blade is customary for most of the older traditions but in the current social climate, where knife culture is regarded as a threat, the urban witch would be ill-advised to carry anything that might be classed as an offensive weapon. A traditional blade has always had a practical purpose, and a suggestion might be to invest in a good Swiss Army knife … it might not have the cachet of a bejewelled-handled athame but at least it won't fall to bits under pressure, or get you arrested.

Here's another 17th century charm where the witch's knife comes into its own, but hardly one that would be acceptable to Social Services, if they have a habit of dropping by for a surprise visit.

Charm

Let the superstitious wife
Near the child's heart lay a knife,
Point be up and half be down;
While she gossips in the town,
This, 'mongst other mystic charms,
Keeps the sleeping child from harm

Whenever we read books containing text and pictures relating to the 'witch's altar', we see a variable clutter of objects that are supposed to be symbolic of Craft. As a result, the esoteric shops are laughing all the way to the bank due to the ever-increasing sales of pretty crystals and other ritual equipment. In the good old days, witches would have utilised whatever household items came to hand for several good reasons:

- They wouldn't want to draw attention to themselves

- They didn't have to impress anyone

- They couldn't afford expensive 'tools'

- There was nowhere to acquire them

- Possession of a jewelled chalice or athame would probably have them arrested for theft

- They didn't need them anyway.

Expensive equipment won't increase magical ability although it can act as an aid for psycho-drama should the occasion demand it. I'm the first to admit that using beautiful and/or antique tools gives a great deal of pleasure, especially if they have been acquired solely for magical purposes. But ... and this is the important thing to understand ... we use them for our *own* benefit not because they are a necessary part of a magical working. If *you* need the psycho-drama, then so be it, but don't for one moment believe that Craft magic is dependant on such trifles.

One of the saddest occasions of my magical 'career' was being asked by the family to help clear a deceased witch's home of its magical paraphernalia before the house clearance people went in. The reasoning behind this request, was that I would recognised what was a ritual item and, even more importantly, how to dispose of it. I could recall the awesome presence of this person in Circle, together with the magnificence of the altar but in the cold, light of day, things were very different. Bereft of their owner's glamour it was just a motley assortment of hand-painted plaster statues; tatty home-made robes; worn dishes, dented chalices and plastic fair-ground jewellery.

The shabbiness of the items didn't in anyway detract from their magical importance but it was an important lesson in what can happen to a witch's possessions if inadequate provision is made for their disposal. The clearance people would have taken the lot down to the local tip, or sold it off as a box of 'curios'. My entire collection is confined to a lockable leather case, with an instruction in my will for the case to be given to a trusted witch-friend for disposal. It's a point to ponder ...

Magical correspondences

More important than acquiring magical equipment is an under-standing of magical correspondences. The formal Tables of Correspondences actually belong to the paths of ritual magic but the practice of linking 'like with like' is an age-old Craft technique. In his classic study of magic, *The Complete Magic Primer*, David Conway wrote that magic, like playing the violin, is something you have to work at. *"Unless you learn first to cope with the scales and simple pieces, you will never tackle the great sonatas."*

Magical correspondences refer to the colours, perfumes, planetary and zodiacal symbols, flora and fauna, times and tides etc., that link our subconscious with the astral realms. In other words, they are esoteric shorthand for conveying occult symbolism between the worlds in much the same way that we are taught to read by pictures when we are small. Let's take the letter 'A' for Apple, for example:

In the magical practitioner's mind, the symbol of the **Apple** would equate with the goddess **Venus/Aphrodite** (remember the 'Judgement of Paris'?), whose colours are **Pink** or **Green**. Also the planet **Venus** corresponds with **Friday**; the zodiacal signs of **Taurus** and **Libra**; the minerals **Copper/Bronze** and gemstones **Jade/Lapis Lazuli**. Flora and fauna are represented by **Apple/Sycamore**, **Rose/Carnation** and the **Dove**. A magical working carried out under the auspices of Venus would relate to harmony, growth and development as well as love and marriage. It also extends to the affections, dance and music, fashion, materialism, personal finances and pleasure.

Therefore the spell for any of these would need to utilise as many of the listed correspondences as possible ... plus a few personal additions of our own. And all this from a humble apple!

This is, of course, a very elementary glimpse into the relativity of correspondences in magical practice. Even the most basic candle spell with its different coloured candles and perfumed anointing oil, is drawing on the symbolism of correspondence, no matter how nicely its been tarted up in the text! The more we understand about magical correspondences, the less we will need to rely on superfluous 'magical' equipment.

Chanting

The use of rhythmic chanting is another important 'tool' for heightening magical intensity. Those of us confined to our urban homes have little chance of raising magical energy by ecstatic dancing but perfecting the art of 'voiceless' chanting can still produce the desired effect. Unfortunately, many of the examples given in contemporary spell books lack the basic ingredients needed to help a witch latch on to her contacts.

That basic ingredient is 'rhythm'. Or to use its dictionary definition: *regular reoccurrence of long and short sounds; a pattern of reoccurrence.* Much of what passes for contemporary chants tend to be a) long screeds of sycophantic toadying to whichever deity is being invoked, and b) excruciatingly bad verse. The secret is to use 'the art of the poet' ... *a composition of high beauty of thought or language and artistic form, typically, but not necessarily, in verse.* And where better to find this, than among the classic poets such as Robert Herrick, William Blake, W B Yeats, Walter de la Mare, Ben Jonson, etc., whose works are often cited as being rooted in the sacred.

Most of the verses featured in *Traditional Witchcraft for Urban Living* have been taken from Robert Herrick's *Hesperides*, a 17th century source quoted extensively by Robin Skelton and Margaret Blackwood in their *Earth, Air, Fire, Water ... pre-Christian and Pagan Elements in British Songs, Rhymes and Ballads.* These verses may not be to everyone's taste, although they are relevant to the language of the period when witchcraft was a common topic amongst the populace.

If chanting isn't to your taste, an alternative is to find suitable pieces of music that can be set to 'repeat' on most CD players. Played at a discreet volume, music can serve a double purpose for the urban witch of a) masking extraneous noises, and b) creating the right atmosphere. In addition to most Gregorian chants and 'O Fortuna' from Carl Orf's *Carmina Burana*, the following suggestions are some I find particularly useful:

"Santos" from *The Armed Man: Mass for Peace* by Karl Jenkins.

"Pie Jesu" from *Requiem* by Karl Jenkins

1492 Conquest of Paradise by Blake, on the album of the same name.

"Cursum Perficio" or "The Longships" from the *Watermark* album by Enya

Daphnis & Chloe (orchestral recording) by Maurice Ravel.

"Foundations of Stone" from *The Two Towers: The Lord of the Rings* trilogy

'Tacoma Trailer' from the Leonard Cohen album, *The Future*

Exercise:

Compile your own personal collection of poems/chants and atmospheric music. Most public libraries have a section for lending tapes/CDs, so you can make your selection at leisure without spending a fortune. Similarly, borrow a variety of both classic and contemporary poetry books, and make a working selection from the poems that 'speak' to you. You don't need to use whole poems or verses – just a repetitive couple of lines that will produce a rhythm all of their own. Keep the details of your selection in a Magical Journal, which will act as a record for your own personal Craft notes.

As we can see, magical 'tools' aren't necessarily anything that can be bought from our local occult shop. The true witch *needs* nothing that has been commercially manufactured to practice his or her Craft. The choice to add a certain amount of regalia to a magical working is a personal one, and not one dictated by what we read in books and magazine articles telling us what we must have.

Chapter Seven – Developing the 'Art of Seeing'

Since the beginning of civilisation, people have always wanted to see into the future – from kings and emperors to the humblest serving wench or farm labourer. Hundreds of recorded British customs and superstitions all have their roots in spells and charms, and they are as fashionable today as they were way back then. It's been said that divination was as commonplace in the past as satellite communication is today: it was part of everyday life.

Eva Shaw comments on its continued popularity in her *Book of Divining the Future*, in that more than ever, men and women consult psychics, mystics, metaphysical therapists and others *'to help solve some of the mysteries of life in these turbulent times ...'* The metaphysical sections of high street bookshops have expanded steadily, not to mention the new age stores specialising in the sales of rune stones, Tarot cards, crystals and astrological charts.

Our old friend Thomas Culpeper has never been more popular. Despite him being the son of a clergyman, modern pagans see the London-based Culpeper as 'one of us' because of his reputation for offering plant-based medicines to his less affluent customers; often telling them where the appropriate plant could be found in the countryside and how it could be collected. He preferred English plants, with their common names and his decision to publish the *London Dispensatory* was taken because those currently in print were based on Latin and included too many imported (and more expensive) drugs. We should not lose sight of the fact, however, that he also lived at a time when astrology had taken on an almost religious overtone, and much of his treatment of disease and ailments was based on astrological calculations, but as one cynic recently wrote: "Only the imprudent would follow his dictates today without question".

Nevertheless, the art of divination and wort-lore are ideal starting points for the urban witch because they need very few 'props' and relatively no psycho-drama to enhance the proceedings. This, however, is only a small part of the witch's stock in trade and although an introduction to the subject can be learned from books, proficiency will only come through practice. The urban witch has an added advantage, in that most towns still have a public library and this can be an extremely valuable asset … not to mention access to a larger number of bookshops catering for pagan interests. For the *real* witch, the pursuit of information (i.e. knowledge) becomes part of the quest.

Divination is the prediction of future events, or the 'discovery of secret matters by a great variety of means, signs and occult techniques', but before a witch can perform this successfully, we need to develop the art of 'seeing'. Often described as being 'both a blessing and a curse', the gift of sight or seeing, is not necessarily confined to witches, and neither is the future fixed.

This A-Z of divination and its attendant meditational techniques by no means includes all the various methods that have been used throughout the centuries. Those listed are the most popular and most suitable for a beginner to try, since they do not require flocks of chickens (alectromancy), entrails (epatoscomancy) or excrement (scatoscopy).

- **Astrology:** the study of the placement of planets and stars at the time of birth.

- **Bibliomancy:** using a sacred book to forecast the future or to provide answers to a question.

- **Cartomancy:** using a pack of cards to predict the future or to respond to a question.

- **Dowsing:** used to search for hidden objects, springs, precious metals, etc., using dowsing sticks or rods.

- **Empyromancy:** interpreting the smoke generated by burning laurel leaves.

- **Felidomancy:** through the observation of feline behaviour.

- **Gematria:** through translating words or sentences into numbers.

- **Hydromancy:** staring at water and interpreting what is seen in it.

- **I-Ching**: or *The Book of Changes* is a system of divination composed of 64 three-line patterns selected by tossing coins.

- **Jungism:** the understanding of mythic symbolism as it relates to human consciousness.

- **Kelidomancy**: the use of a suspended object in order to foretell the future or to respond to a question.

- **Leconomancy**: the movement of oil pored into water.

- **Meditation:** a controlled state of higher awareness during which the seeker concentrates on a word or idea in order to receive guidance.

- **Nephelomancy:** using the patterns seen in cloud formation.

- **Omens**: unusual activities, occurrences or events used to divine the future.

- **Palmistry**: studying the shape and size of the hand, along with analysis of the lines, mounts, skin colour and finger length.

- **Qabbala**: a blend of powerful God-inspired divination and mysticism.

- **Rhabdomancy**: divining for water or precious stones using rods or wands.

- **Sciomancy**: the size and shape of shadows.

- **Tasseography:** the ritual reading of tealeaves or coffee grounds.

- **Uromancy:** divination using urine.

- **Visualisation:** a controlled level of consciousness during which the seeker can divine answers to questions.

- **Wore-Lore**: the understanding of appropriate herbs to use to aid divination.

- **Xylomancy:** using the arrangement of dried sticks.

- **Yoga**: both a form of meditation and a practical discipline

- **Zoanthropy:** observing and interpreting the flames of three lighted candles placed in a triangular position.

The classic occult encyclopaedia, *Man, Myth & Magic*, makes a very valid observation on the subject, which we would do well to remember: that the most remarkable thing about divination is its continued success! Even stripping away the material and highly lucrative aspects, even the most hardened cynic would have to admit that for the art to 'survive ecclesiastical condemnation, and the gibes of rationalists and sceptics', it has had to come up with the goods on a regular basis.

It is also important to accept that no-one can excel at all the different methods, and that it is best to develop one particular system that produces the best results *for you*. Experienced practitioners often prefer to use a single form of divination, 'immersing themselves in the method and spiritual tradition of that form'. Some methods may prove to be more efficient than others, and some diviners my be more accurate than their fellows, but it is an important aspect of a witch's natural ability to be able to divine by 'rod, bird and finger', as the saying goes.

Nevertheless, whatever method is used to predict the future, those results are not cast in stone! Divination reveals the future as relating to the past and the present, and what will happen if the warnings are not heeded in order to change things *before* they go wrong. The answer is also subjective to where an individual is standing at the precise moment in time at which they pose the question.

We're back to the saying: *"You can't change anything but yourself, but in changing yourself, everything changes around you."* For example: the chaotic imagery of The Tower, or the Death card doesn't mean that your house is about to fall down, or that you should open a dialogue with the local undertaker. Both are warnings that sudden or unexpected changes are about to occur – so watch out! The direction of the trouble or change will be influenced by the cards on either side, which give you 'intelligence' of the evasive or preparatory action you need to take. Divination is a useful tool for making sure you always make the right decisions and I never undertake any important step without consulting the Tarot!

Importance of correspondences in divination

Omens are signs of opportunities to be taken, dangers to be avoided, or impending news of change. Here the witch interacts with Nature to keep close watch on any unusual activities or occurrences that might have any effect on themselves, or those close to them. This is another reason why it is essential for even urban witches to be well-versed in nature-lore as well as magical correspondences. It pays to understand the local wildlife, otherwise we might not see that unusual 'something' in an animal's or bird's normal behaviour patterns.

Our native flora and fauna are linked to our magical subconscious and, if we have used any form of divinational methods to guide us through the next stages of our love, life or career, we must be receptive to the responses. For those with a working understanding in the language of correspondences, it is easy to grasp how natural the reading of the symbols becomes, and how easy and obvious (in most instances) is the interpretation. For the beginner, however, accept that the answers are not going to appear suddenly like the writing on the wall, foreshowing downfall and disaster at Belshazzar's feast. Divination is more subtle and, more often than not for the inexperienced, irritatingly obtuse!

According to Carl Jung, the primitive psyche of man borders on the life of the 'animal soul' and it is at this level we find the Collective Unconscious, a stratum of mental patterns (i.e. archetypal symbols) common to all people, anywhere in the world. This is the subjective home of many mythic and hereditary elements of primordial imagery, and explains why it is necessary to have an understanding of mythic symbolism as it relates to human consciousness.

On a much more mundane level than Jung's exalted teachings, we need to get used to interpreting the images we receive from our subconscious via our divination techniques. Books will give a basic introduction to the subject of magical correspondences but in reality, interpreting the signs and symbols is more like word-association and differ considerably from person to person. Your correspondences will not be mine; both of us may differ from the example given in the books. Let us say, for example, that I've received the impression of a deer in the tealeaves or crystal ball.

What does the deer symbolise? For starters, the animal has been associated with deities from just about every pantheon on the planet ... which doesn't help unless we've been working specifically with the Horned God, or Diana/Artemis (moon) energies and the deity's appearance is the answer we require. I don't have any connection to Hindu or Japanese mythology, so I'm instinctively going to look closer to home.

What about the animal itself? The 'hart and the hind' were considered by the Elizabethan nobility to be two of the five 'beasts of venery' (also including the boar, wolf and hare) and the only quarry worthy of the chase. The image also plays a prominent part in heraldry, so I'm probably not looking at a *domestic* situation. I need to think 'outside the box' and try to visualise a position where *I would be a quarry worth pursing*. If it's nothing to do with home or family, what about career/business? Is someone trying to out-manoeuvre me on this level? Do I have an undisclosed enemy in the workplace?

What is the animal telling me? Be alert and watchful. Flight or fight. The deer is swift of foot and can outrun (out-manoeuvre) the hounds, but a stag at bay is a dangerous animal to confront. Lateral thinking is the secret of a good divination technique.

How do I know if my interpretation is right, and I'm not off in cloud-cuckoo-land with my imagination running riot? This is where we interact with Nature and look for the signs. The urban witch won't encounter the *Monarch of the Glen,* but she might just find the tiny hoof prints of a muntjac next day when out walking the dog. Many of these small deer live on motorway banks, factory grounds, wasteland and Ministry of Defence restricted areas, particularly in the South East and Midlands. They have even been known to take shelter in garden sheds and outhouses in bad weather. So, having received confirmation that our process of elimination is correct, we can ascertain where the possible threat is coming from in the physical world and be on our guard.

Cards and Crystals

For most witches, the most popular forms of divination are probably the Tarot and the crystal ball. The choice of Tarot deck is a very personal one and must be acquired by intuition rather than recommendation. The designs vary widely from the old Marseilles (French) or traditional Rider Waite packs, to a whole range of contemporary pictorial offerings ... choose the version that 'speaks' to you personally. There are no standard pictures or presentation, and even the attributes, may vary from deck to deck.

A full Tarot pack consists of 78 cards: 56 cards of the minor arcana divided into four suits of wands, clubs, pentacles and cups and 22 trumps of the major arcana. The major arcana consists of universal archetypal symbols, and each card equates with a particular 'path' on the Qabalistic 'Tree of Life' ... which can be used as meditational doorways to specific areas of the Tree at a later stage. Familiarise ourselves with the archetypes represented and we won't go far wrong in beginning to learn the esoteric meaning of the cards. For example:

0 The Fool

The universal concept of the Trickster, who is a subtle blend of innocence and cunning, like the eternal child.

I The Magus
The Magician of myth and legend, who is also our mentor and guide.

II Priestess
The Wise Woman and the female counterpart of the Hierophant, who instructs in the art of occult knowledge.

III Empress
The beneficent Queen and the epitome of charity and kindness.

IV Emperor
A great King, a wise and powerful ruler: all that is positive in the masculine persona.

V Hierophant
The Teacher who imparts esoteric knowledge to the people, in a practical and oral way they can understand.

VI The Lovers
Represents the alchemical Union of man and woman on all levels. Yin and Yang.

VII Chariot
A martial symbol of Victory in the face of overwhelming odds.

VIII Strength
The inner Strength that can unexpectedly come to the surface in the most unlikely of persons or situations.

IX Hermit
Signifies the silence surrounding Inner Knowledge and that which must be sought after.

X Wheel of Fortune
A change of Fortune or circumstances - and usually for the better.

XI Justice
Equilibrium. The concept of Justice being tempered with Mercy; and Mercy tempered with Justice.

XII Hanged Man
Redemption through sacrifice and submission to the Divine Will; as in the universal myth of the sacrificial god.

XIII Death
In esoteric terms, the Passing from one stage to another; the universal link between material and spiritual.

XIV Temperance
Personal Control over an indulgence of the natural appetites and passions.

XV Devil
The card is often referred to as Pan, and the force of unbridled Nature.

XVI Tower
The symbolic Destruction of all that is important/prominent … but not always in a negative form.

XVII Star
The symbol of timeless Mystery and the ever-turning cosmos.

XVIII Moon
The archetypal suggestion of Illusion, often representing standing on the brink of important change.

XIX Sun
The ultimate symbol of Light, warmth and strength.

XX Judgement
Final decision concerning the past and a new current for the future. Life progressing a little further along the Path.

XXI Universe
Representing the macrocosm and the microcosm – All.

A Tarot deck usually comes with its own booklet giving details of suggested layouts (or spread) and the traditional interpretation of the cards, both in the upright and reversed positions. Ultimately the cards will speak to you – but the messages may not be those given in the popular books. Begin by working solely with the major arcana and become completely familiar with the design of each card. Eventually one will have a stronger 'voice' than the rest and this will become *your* card, regardless of the representation or traditional interpretation. Drawing this card will always have a special significance for you alone, and can be used as a personal gateway for visualisation and meditation.

The more familiar you become with the Tarot, the easier it will be for you to interpret the signs and become a competent reader. The basic archetypal associations given above are but one of the many meanings behind each design, and we have to learn to how to read that intricate multi-layering. Not just of the card itself, but also its relationship to the other cards in the spread. The positioning of one card, for example, may negate the influence of its neighbour – for better or worse – but the more levels of the magical onion we unravel, we realise just how *little* we know. The Tarot has a remarkable knack of putting folk in their place!

Exercise:

Begin to find your way around the Tarot by starting with a simple three-card spread. Ask the question to which you need an answer as you shuffle the cards of the major arcana. Fan the cards in your left hand and extract one at random with the right ... place it face up in front of you. Now draw the second card and place face up to the left of the first card. Now draw the third card and place face up on the right of the first card.

Spiritual	Response	Earthly
Mental	Answer	Practical
Unconscious	Result	Material

The middle card represents the basic response to the question and using the booklet accompanying your deck, find the corresponding interpretation. The card on the left represents the spiritual/intellectual influences on the response; while the card on the right, affects the temporal side of things, depending on whether the cards are reversed (i.e up-side- down) or right way up. The booklet will guide you along the path of reading your first Tarot spread ... but don't frighten yourself to death if the cards appear all doom and gloom! It's only an exercise.

Although there is a popular craze for shop-bought rocks and crystals, those with the greatest magical potency are the ones we locate ourselves. Our world is built of rocks, minerals and crystals, and we can go rock hunting *anywhere*. As the traditional witch was more likely to use a local piece of stone as a power object or amulet, it makes sense to begin our search nearer home. Neither is it necessary to possess a detailed knowledge of geology to collect 'magical' pebbles because a small stone that catches our eye due to its unusual colour or shape, will influence our choice. And good pebbles *are* to be found anywhere ... the shallow stream bed in the park, on the tow-path of the canal, dug up in the garden, or even among gravel used on building sites and landscaped areas.

We may discover a special stone under unusual circumstances, or it may be something that we feel the urge to pick up and possess. Having come straight from the Earth, how much more potent and personal this small stone will be, rather than an expensive polished crystal that has been commercially mined and prepared for the high street 'Crystal Cave'.

Quartz is one of the most common 'crystals', and pebbles having quartz as their dominant constituent are to be found everywhere. Quartz crystals, however, are unique because their inner and outer aspects are identical: the only known structures on the planet to exhibit this characteristic. And did you know that quartz is solid silica ... if it didn't crystallise when it solidified, it became flint? Now, everyone knows that two flints struck together will produce a spark, but it is not generally known that *all* quartz pebbles will do the same ... and often produce bigger and better sparks. Clear quartz or rock crystal, will produce an orange spark if two pieces are struck together in a darkened room, together with a smell of burning. This makes them ideal for the working of magic in a dual Earth/Fire capacity, but they are often overlooked as they appear plain when placed next to some of the more exotic and colourful crystals.

Physics and fortune-tellers throughout the ages have used crystal balls and shewstones to divine the future. Today, as often as not the 'crystal' ball will be made from moulded glass and this is a poor imitation of the real thing. The *real* thing is of polished rock crystal, and one of the most famous being the smokey-quartz shewstone that belonged to Dr John Dee that is now in the British Museum. The crystal ball has been around for a long time: in 5th century Ireland there was a Guild of crystal gazers known as the Specularii, but most authorities appear to agree that the practice had its origins in Persia.

The following is based on instruction from an early journal of occultism, *Borderland,* and reproduced in a 1935 edition of *The Book of Fortune Telling,* describing the use of a traditional crystal ball in what is probably the best, no-nonsense view of the subject, and divided the crystal vision into three separate manifestations:

1 Images of things unconsciously observed;

2 Images of ideas unconsciously acquired;

3 Images clairvoyant or prophetic.

"Clear rock crystal is the prime material for making crystal balls, and the object is generally to concentrate on the points of light reflected from the sphere. Continued for any length of time, that procedure will gradually induce a state of self-hypnosis, and then the act of crystal gazing can properly begin. Many accounts state that the gazer suddenly finds that the globe has disappeared, and has been replaced by a veil of mist upon which the visions come and go."

Exercise:
If you are fortunate enough to acquire a true crystal ball, here are a few good, old-fashioned tips to help you get started:

• Its owner should only handle the crystal.

• A black silk handkerchief should be folded around the crystal to prevent reflection.

• Frequent passes made with the right hand gives power to the crystal.

• Passes made with the left hand give it 'sensitivity'.

- Clouds that appear in the crystal are good omens if they are white, violet, green or blue, but inauspicious if black, red or yellow.

- Ascending clouds answer any question in the affirmative; descending clouds answer in the negative.

- Appearances in the right side of the crystal are of mundane earthly origin; those on the left are symbolic or psychic images.

Needless to say, the apparitions that appear in the crystal are going to be those infuriatingly obtuse images but it's a magical reality, that the language of correspondences has always communicated itself in the form of allegory, symbol and metaphor. There are, however, other methods of using crystals or stones for divination, which are less costly, and often easier to read.

Lithomancy, using precious and semi-precious stones, cut or uncut, is possibly one of the oldest forms of foretelling the future or interpreting omens, either by:

Casting of Lots
Using this method requires specific crystals (or stones) being cast onto a circle, marked out with divisions for emotions and advice. The 'lots' are deciphered according to the influence of the stone and its placement within the circle. You can use either 12 similar sized stones that correspond with the signs of the zodiac (birthstones), or 10 that correspond with the spheres of the Tree of Life (11 if you count Daath).

Remember that many of the 'birthstones' are given as precious gems, and few of us can afford to own diamonds, sapphires, rubies and emeralds to roll around the floor. You can collect your own stones, providing you can assign different attributes to each individual one ... and remember what they are during a casting session!

or

Scrying

This is a method of studying a single gem or crystal, and interpreting the images or suggestions generated by the stone. As with crystal balls, the crystal is placed in a quiet area, and a light source is reflected off the natural sides, or the facets of a cut stone. Through studying and interpreting the play of light, images seen in the stone, or ideas unconsciously acquired, the answer to your question will be revealed

According to *Magical Jewels of the Middle Ages and the Renaissance*, an emerald is the most effective gemstone for divinational (or 'foreshadowing things to come') purposes ... but it also 'makes its wearer eloquent and persuasive; is a cure for epilepsy and semi-tertian fever; it rests the eyes and averts tempests'. Perhaps, it's best to stick with a quartz crystal!

Visualisation and Lucid Dreaming

At its most basic, visualisation is the ability to form and hold a series of pictures in the mind's eye. On a more advanced level it could be described as controlled thought projection of a magical journey or scenario in which we *consciously* take part. The technique is an intrinsic part of almost all modern magical practice, and is often used in the early stages as a spring-board for a deeper path-working, divination or meditation.

David Conway, in *Secret Wisdom*, described the technique as conditioning the mind to be as supple as the body of a well-trained gymnast. Unfortunately, the concept of visualisation and path-working has been 'dumbed-down' in recent years to such an extent that some will accept the former as being genuine path-working. In traditional teaching, visualisation is merely looked upon as a controlled exercise at the lower end of the psychic exercise scale. So, let's use our imagination ...

Let's imagine a walk along the seashore. It can be a favourite bay where you've walked the dog; a childhood memory of holidays at the seaside; a white sandy beach on the Maldives ... or a completely imaginary place. We 'see' it in our mind's eye. We follow the moving pictures as we *consciously* follow the story-line we're creating. As we become more proficient, we will even be able to smell and taste the saltiness in the sea air, and feel the breeze blowing off the waves.

From here we progress into path-working, which is an astral journey for the purpose of magical or divinational instruction. Here the practitioner has no control over the outcome or sequence of events. One moment we are on the beach and the next ... who knows where the astral gulf stream will take us? This state is usually reached *via* visualisation, where the practitioner sets the scene on a conscious level, and then allows themselves to be drawn into an involuntary journey of discovery or revelation.

The elementary exercise for perfecting visualisation techniques is to concentrate on a simple object or pattern. Then, with the eyes shut, recreate the image inside your head. Earlier in this chapter we looked at finding 'your' card in the Tarot deck, which we referred to as a personal gateway for visualisation and meditation. Sit comfortably in a relaxed atmosphere and place the chosen card directly in front of you. Stare at the image and try to re-create the picture inside your head with all the details intact. Some Tarot decks are more intricate than others, and so the exercise will require more mental effort. When you feel you have 'visualised' every detail, try to see the picture from another angle other than a full-frontal image.

Once you have achieved this result, you may find that you are drawn *through* the card and out onto the astral. All too often, however, these techniques are used to produce a psychic 'feel good trip' with no magical or divinatory purpose in mind, but when we're in the learning stages there does seem to be a protective barrier to prevent us from coming to harm. On the other hand, once we become proficient, we're on the high wire alone and without a safety net!

When attempting any of these exercises we must always remember that our skills and abilities will improve dramatically with regular practice, and that five to ten minutes every day is far more effective than doing a full hour's work once a week. Neither is there any point in trying an exercise on a couple of occasions and thinking: "Oh, I've done that one. Let's forget about it and go onto something else." Craft is not a cabaret act for our own personal amusement, it is drawing on a natural energy with its own set of rules – learn the rules and in time the discipline will pay off because we will eventually learn, not to break them, but how to take short-cuts.

If the visualisation and path-working exercises seem a bit too daunting, then there is a simple method of divination that might be a better approach to begin with – lucid dreaming. This is a half-waking, half-dream state where we are fully conscious and aware of our surroundings, but still able to receive images or impressions from the astral. The astral image is often superimposed over the immediate surroundings, like a double-exposure on a photograph.

I've always found this method highly useful when looking for the answer to a problem. Believe it or not, it is best performed in the daytime, preferably on a sunny day. Sit in a chair or on the floor in a patch of sunlight where it comes through the window. Place a lighted candle in the sunlit area and stare into the flame, which will become almost invisible in the sunshine. Think of the problem that needs resolving and as you stare at the flame, you will feel yourself slipping into a light semi-hypnotic state. At the same time you will be fully conscious of what's going on around you. In this psychic 'slip-stream' I would be very surprised if the appropriate messages don't come filtering through.

To repeat what our old friend, *Man, Myth & Magic* says: the most remarkable thing about divination is its overwhelming success.

Chapter Eight – Green Peace

When I sat down to begin this chapter there were lots of conflicting ideas running around. It would have been easy to compile a list of things a witch *should* grow in her garden but, like life, it ain't that simple. Urban witches are usually pushed for space, so how to tackle the problem of creating our own magical green patch with the minimum amount of room? Then I looked at the outdoor plants that have followed me around throughout the years ... and provided me with a lot of pleasure and continuity.

Through necessity I've had to perfect the art of what is known as 'container gardening', simply because it's easier to lug pots around, rather than keep digging everything up, and possibly killing it off in the process. My 'permanent' display consists of a pedestal urn planted with thyme, surrounded by an assortment of pots and containers of all shapes, textures and sizes. In these I grow lavender, mint, rosemary, sage, miniature comfrey, parsley and violets. There are another half dozen larger containers that hold the bay tree, an azalea, star magnolia, camellia and two very large aspidistra.

This collection has lived successively (and successfully) on a sunny patio; a gravelled drive; in a walled yard; a narrow front garden and on a balcony. Admittedly herbs do need sun to thrive and this should be the first consideration when positioning your containers. When space is restricted, the design of that space becomes all-important, although *A Witch's Treasury for Hearth & Garden* tells us that a canny witch will utilise every nook and cranny for growing things, even if you don't have so much as a patio or yard. *"Even a small space can give a witch space to 'be' and your neighbours will think nothing if they see you sitting on the step with a coffee, or relaxing in a garden chair in your special corner. Being a witch doesn't mean that you have to make grand ritual gestures to follow your beliefs – a quiet corner prepared with loving care is the only sacred space you need."*

What's your problem?

Lack of space? Or lack of imagination? We can't all apply ourselves with the dexterity (and cheque book) of the *Ground Force* team, but we can utilise what little space we've got. Many herbs are cultivated for their beauty as well as their medicinal and culinary uses, and have been an attractive feature in ornamental gardens for centuries.

So … just how *small* is the space available for growing things? Is it not much wider than a side alley four feet deep? Is it a tiny yard, or a balcony area barely large enough for a plant pot? No matter how small the area, think of it as an integral part of your home that can be enhanced to provide some green peace in the middle of a city. By exploring the imagination, a witch can create her own outdoor environment with just a bit of careful planning – and at very low cost. An entire herb garden can be planted in an assortment of pots and containers, providing they allow for drainage. But do bear in mind, however, that ungated front gardens can invite the neighbour-hood dogs to cock a leg over the pots – which will not enhance the magical properties of the herbs or their flavour!

So … before dashing off to the local garden centre, mark the four cardinal points – or quarters – using a compass. Remember, if its big enough to stand in, it's big enough to use magically, so think about how you can create a sacred area that will mean nothing to any inquisitive over-lookers. And before you decide that wind-chimes would be perfect for representing Elemental Air, be warned that a couple were threatened with prosecution when council officials ruled that their wind chimes were causing noise pollution, following complaints from the neighbours!

Let's keep it simple and begin with those herbs commonly in domestic use: such as the familiar herbs listed in the traditional folk song, *Scarborough Fair* – 'parsley, sage, rosemary and thyme' – since to get us started, all can be obtained ready-grown in pots from a local supermarket or garden centre. We can always expand our collection at a later stage, as our magical needs increase. As we discussed in Chapter One, experiment and get a *feel* for the plant. These particular herbs have been around for a very long time. Parsley, is still used as a digestive aid, and was said to 'take away bitterness': medieval doctors prescribing it for spiritual maladies as well. Sage has been a symbol of strength for thousands of years; while rosemary represents faithfulness, love and remembrance. Thyme symbolises courage, and during the Middle Ages ladies presented their 'favours' embroidered with a sprig of thyme to their chosen knight.

Parsley: Planetary association: Mercury
Culinary: Rich in vitamins A and C. The leaves are used as garnish and to flavour sauces, butters, dressings, stuffings and savoury dishes.
Medicinal: Used to sooth menstrual complaints, cystitis, anaemia and arthritis. Chewed raw, the leaves act as a breath-freshener, especially after eating garlic or onions.
Folk-lore: The plant was said to grow well in a garden where the woman was the dominant partner.
Magical: Protective and has a calming effect. Good for health and money spells.
Sentiment: Entertainment, feasting.

Sage: Planetary association: Venus
Culinary: A strong aromatic herb traditionally used in vinegars, wines, liqueurs and ales as well as stuffings, soups and pickles.
Medicinal: Has antiseptic properties, making it an ideal mouthwash and gargle for ulcers and sore throats.
Folk-lore: Reputed to aid longevity, and where it flourished in

a garden, the owner's business would prosper.

Magical: Protection and attracting money. Good for cleansing the home of negative vibes.

Sentiment: Domestic virtue.

Rosemary: Planetary association: Sun

Culinary: Use for flavouring fish and meat, particularly lamb.

Medicinal: Being antibacterial and antifungal, it is used externally for eczema, sores and wounds. Also used as a hair tonic.

Folk-lore: Placed under the pillow at night, rosemary was said to ward off evil spirits and bad dreams.

Magical: Protection and improving the memory. Good for love spells.

Sentiment: Remembrance

Thyme: Planetary association: Venus

Culinary: Stimulates the appetite and helps the digestion.

Medicinal: Useful lotion for thrush, athlete's foot and other fungal infections.

Folk-lore: Bunches of thyme were burned to fumigate houses and repel insects.

Magical: Helps to focus energy and prepare for magical working.

Sentiment: Activity, courage.

Now let's look at where we can grow them:

Balconies

In modern blocks of flats, balconies tend to be designed on a uniform plan, often overshadowed by the floor above and certainly not suitable for the excessive weight of heavy containers filled with compost. Usually the area is too small for sitting out, but clever planting in lightweight containers can provide constant greenery to be enjoyed from *inside* the flat. Even the smallest balcony can accommodate one or two pots for culinary herbs.

Examine the possibilities of positioning hanging baskets on the walls or suspended from the overhead beams if these exist – exploit the vertical space available as much as you can. If the balcony catches the full sun, plants will still need to be hardy in order to stand up to the exposure; but container planting allows you to move your herbs into shade, or out of the wind. It is also important not to overcrowd a container because herbs need ample 'elbow room' to grow.

All of the 'Scarborough Four' would suit balcony planting as it's possible to get trailing varieties of rosemary and thyme. The three varieties of sage (common, purple and tricolour) could also be planted together for effect. Parsley can be grown in small separate pots; sown in rotation to provide a continuous supply. Add mint to the collection but keep it in a container on its own as it spreads like wild-fire and strangles everything in its path.

Window Boxes

If you want to grow herbs in a window box, remember that they need full sun and constant watering. Although plastic boxes don't have the same appeal as terracotta or wood, they are much easier to move and retain moisture well. Cover the base with an inch of stones or broken crocks, and cover with a layer of potting compost. Keep perennial herbs in their pots to protect the roots when the annuals need replacing.

Place the herbs in their pots in the container and fill the remaining space with compost. Always position tall plants at the back of the box. Plant any annuals directly into the compost between the perennials, making sure that the roots are well covered. Press down firmly around the base of the herb with your fingertips in order to anchor the roots in the soil. Water the newly planted window box to help the herbs settle in and mature.

A suitable selection for a window box includes seven of the most popular culinary herbs. All are reasonably hardy perennials (chives, bay, sage, rosemary and marjoram) except for parsley and summer savory. Replant the window box when the plants become crowded.

Do remember that any kind of window box, hanging basket or tub will demand constant attention for the plants are entirely dependent on your care. Out in an open garden they can spread their roots in search of nourishment, but in the narrow confines of a container they must be provided with everything they need. And don't forget that little rain falls straight down, so even in wet weather window boxes and tubs may receive little or no natural watering.

Kitchen window sill

The kitchen window sill usually provides the best mini-greenhouse for growing pot-herbs for culinary use. The only limiting factors are the size of the plants and the length of time that any herb can be kept in good condition in lower light levels.

Add sweet majoram, chives and applemint to the four favourites for variety. It's also possible to buy purpose-made colourful ceramic pots with a matching drip tray for holding those herbs bought from the supermarket and hiding the plain black plastic tubs in which they usually arrive.

If you're feeling adventurous, also try planting 3-4 watercress shoots in a six-inch pot of rich compost, standing it in water that is changed daily. Pots of seedlings for cutting like salad cress can be bought from the supermarket, while rocket, coriander and dill are especially suitable for cropping as seedlings: rocket seeds sprout within 3-4 days; coriander takes about 5-6 days; and dill within 10 days. And all grow well on a sunny window sill.

Hanging baskets

Space-saving culinary herb baskets can provide additional

growing space, although they dry out quickly, need plenty of watering and a regular supply of plant food. Moisture retention can be improved by adding granules that absorb water. The 'Scarborough Four' can be grown in hanging baskets with nasturtiums for colour – or add savory and basil for variety.

Front or back steps

An arrangement of different sized plant pots containing our favourite herbs will provide a welcoming, tiered effect if the pots are grouped in threes or fives. Again, tri-colour and purple sage adds a touch of colour. Terracotta 'strawberry' planters come in all sizes and can be filled with a selection of herbs; or just trailing nasturtiums, the leaves providing a peppery flavour for salads. Planters allow for seasonal flexibility as most of the herbs need replacing regularly.

Filled with suitable plants, this type of planter is also an ideal 'starter' for someone developing an interest in medicinal herbs. The pockets enable a number of herbs to be grown in a small space, which will need to be replanted every spring. An assortment recommended by the Royal Horticultural Society (and several by Thomas Culpeper) consists of lemon verbena, common houseleek, thyme, marigold, aloe vera, feverfew, chamomile, hyssop and mint.

Lemon verbena: No planetary correspondence.
The expensive oil from this plant was once popular in perfumery – the essential oil is both insecticidal and bactericidal. Use dried leaves for infusions for feverish colds and indigestion. **Sentiment: none given.**

Common houseleek: A herb of Jupiter.
The leaves gentle rubbed on the places stung by nettles or bees, will quickly remove the pain. The juice applied daily to a corn will soften it. Often found growing on old roofs as it was

believe to protect the building from lightening strike – hence its magical association with the two thunder-gods, Jupiter and Thor. Charlemagne ordered that the plant be grown throughout his empire for its magical properties, which included keeping evil spirits away. **Sentiment: Vivacity.**

Thyme: A herb of Venus

A natural antiseptic and rich in thymol. It relieves throat and bronchial irritation and the spasms of whooping cough. **Sentiment: Activity, Courage.**

Marigold: A herb of the Sun

A medieval emblem of enduring love. The flowers were used to relieve wasp and bee stings. **Sentiment: Mental anguish**

Aloe vera: No planetary correspondence

Control fungal infection, is anti-inflammatory and promotes healing Use externally for burns, scalds, sunburn, wounds, eczema, and to prevent nail-biting. **Sentiment: Acute sorrow, bitterness.**

Feverfew: A herb of Venus

An effective remedy for headaches and migraine in the form of an infusion; while a tincture applied locally relieves the pain and irritation of insect bites. This herb was listed by Aelfric, a Benedictine monk of Cerne Abbas (c.995-1010). **Sentiment: A clear head.**

Chamomile: A herb of the Sun

An excellent infusion for headaches and migraine, or three drops of chamomile oil on a lump of sugar as an alternative. Bathing with a decoction of the herb takes away weariness and eases aches and pains. Also listed by Aelfric. **Sentiment: Energy in adversity.**

Hyssop: A herb of Jupiter

Mainly used in an infusion as a cough and chest medicine. In ancient times it was used in purifying ceremonies, and in the cleansing of sacred temples. Strewn on the floor of churches and infirmaries, the herb was reputed to prevent the spread of infectious diseases. **Sentiment: Cleanliness.**

Mint: A herb of Venus

According to Culpeper: *'The juice of Garden Mint taken in vinegar, stays bleeding and stirs up venery, or bodily lust'.* Mainly used for culinary purposes but is added to medicines because of its pleasant taste. An infusion of the dried leaves is also excellent for nausea and wind. Watermint was one of the three most sacred herbs of the Druids, the others being meadowsweet and vervain. **Sentiment: Virtue**

Even for the most dedicated of witches, it *is* pointless attempting to grow herbs without direct sunlight, and some sites may be better suited to decorative plants that thrive in the shade. Nature provides vegetation for all locations and plenty of attractive plants thrive in dark areas. According to the RHS, scale must be the first concern of the small garden but this does not mean everything has to be miniature ... *"a tiny space, crammed with bijou furniture, Lilliputian pots and dwarf plants is uncomfortable"* say the experts. And since many really small gardens are in towns, bounded by high walls or sunk down among surrounding tall buildings, they usually have the problem of shade cast by neighbouring buildings and/or high boundary walls.

Side Alleys

With the walls painted white or cream, sunless areas can still be utilised to provide a green cave using different hostas, hydrangea and bamboo, all of which will grow well in shade. Even a dark 'well' can be transformed by using pale colours, luminous in darkness, such as white-flowered honesty, or the white-variegated evergreen euonymus ... *"Bring illusions and light down into the garden"* say the experts.

Brightly coloured plastic pots and containers can also help to transform a dull corner, especially if it isn't suitable for flowers but no matter how gloomy your patch, unusual ferns and ivy can still be used for maximum effect. Although many shade-loving plants may be foreign imports, ivy (ruled by the planet Saturn) is a sacred plant and believed to have protective magical properties, while common ferns (ruled by the planet Mercury) were considered a good treatment for wounds and bruises. Hart's Tongue ferns (ruled by the planet Jupiter) protected against snakebites and passions of the heart!

Walls

If space is at a premium, create a cascade of wall-mounted baskets with trailing plants. This method can be quite effective if there is a descending metal stair going down into an enclosed yard or basement flat. By painting the walls and stairs white, the whole area is given a lift by the use of reflective light. Use wooden decking and pebbles together, as mixed materials work well together in a small space, with the minimum inclusion of foliage.

Bin sheds and coal bunkers

Use the flat surfaces for low-level containers and plant aromatic plants to hide any dustbin smells. Unsightly wheelie bins can also be camouflaged with specially designed 'leaf' covers to blend in with the hedge, or conceal behind a bamboo screen.

These unsightly necessities are usually located at the front of the house right outside the sitting room window, so consider constructing some form of 'cupboard' with a flat roof, which can be used for shallow containers of brightly coloured bedding plants, together with low-growing herbs such as thyme and house leek.

The Doctrine of Signatures

One of the most ancient notions of medicine was what was known as 'the doctrine of signatures', whereby the visual appearance of a plant was often believed to reveal its medicinal uses by its likeness to a part of the body. The theory was simply along the lines of: those plants with yellow sap would be used to treat jaundice, while those with a rough texture would heal all skin complaints. Colours also played an important part in the doctrine and the claims grew more and more extravagant ... and intermingled with the theory of Astrological Botany.

The healers of the 16-17th centuries were full of botanical mysticism. Paracelsus himself opined that each plant was a terrestrial star, and each star a spiritualised plant! Nicholas Culpeper hurled insults at the doctors and herbalists who dared to criticise his methods of using the Zodiac as part of his treatment. As late as 1826, Dr Parkins, author of the *English Physician*, gives tables and instruction for gathering plants and herbs at the appropriate planetary hour and 'How to find the Planetary Hours for each Day in the Week'.

On the surface all this would suggest that incredible flights of fancy were required for such theories. Culpeper wrote: "If you dig up the root of [lesser celandine], you shall perceive the perfect image of that disease which they commonly call the piles," and lesser celandine was often referred to as 'pilewort', meaning the herb for piles. But if we turn to the RHA *Encyclopaedia of Herbs* for a cross-reference, we find that the plant is still used today for treating haemorrhoids!

Not everything in a witch's world has a culinary, medicinal or magical use. We *are* allowed to grow flowers and plants for pure enjoyment. Given that flowers have played an important part in the history, myth, legend and art of the whole of mankind, it is not surprising that there is a great deal of folk-lore lore attached to them, too. Hundreds of species of flora have been attributed with meanings from an obvious symbol to complete messages, and these plant names and their meanings were compiled in specialist dictionaries that sold out, one edition after the other in Europe and America. This lore became known as 'florigraphy' – the language of flowers.

It appears to have been Lady Mary Wortley Montagu who first mentioned the custom in 1717, when she wrote to a friend from Constantinople: "... there is no colour, no flower, no weed, no fruit, herb, pebble, or feather that has not a verse belonging to it ..." The first real flower dictionary, *Le Langage des Fleurs*, by Madame Charlotte de la Tour was published in Paris in 1818, ran to eighteen editions and started the fashion for similar works with beautiful illustrations and engravings. The fashion for these books in England began during the reign of George IV and ran through the early years of Queen Victoria.

Although the authors of the flower dictionaries often cited the Middle Eastern origin for the custom, there does not appear to be any source other than what Lady Mary reported. Henry Phillips, who penned some of the best known British versions, provided some 'genuine scholarship' about the meanings attributed to flowers in folklore and literature but for most, the books were padded out with poetry and classical quotations. As a result, of the 150 known titles, no two agreed completely about the meanings of the flowers, unless one book happened to be plagiarised from another, and even in a single dictionary, a plant might be given three totally different, even contradictory meanings.

A large number of the flowers listed were among those foreign varieties that gathered popularity during the Victorian era, and many of the meanings given reflect the overly religious and romantic sentiments of the period. Should we decide to engage in the 'language of flowers', whether for romantic or other purposes, we must ensure that the recipient has access to the same source material or the gesture could be counter-productive! Few of these plant-meanings will be found in any of the classic herbals, and the significance can differ considerably from the texts of Nicholas Culpeper.

For magical purposes, these flower meanings should not be viewed as genuine 'correspondences' or as part of a traditional witch's wort-lore.

A final word:

A friend of mine lives in a second-floor apartment overlooking a busy high street. There is one large deep-silled window in which she cultivates the most magnificent display of hibiscus – not for any medicinal use but for the sheer joy of watching them bloom. [The flowers can be used to produce a sweet, astringent that checks bleeding, soothes irritated tissues and relaxes spasms.] The plants are under-lit at night, to give the maximum pleasure and this is her 'temple' – a luxurious oasis of green peace in the middle of town.

Ritual for dedicating an area of green peace

Choose a time just after sunset and light a candle in a suitable container – one that will shelter the flame from the wind if the ritual is being performed outside. For this you will need:

- A green candle

- A glass of pure spring water

- A suitable charm

My choice would possibly be this extract from *The Sunken Garden* by Walter de la Mare as follows:

> *Speak not – whisper not;*
> *Here bloweth thyme and bergamot;*
> *Softly on the evening hour*
> *Secret herbs their spices shower,*

Dark-spiked rosemary and myrrh,
Lean-stalked, purple lavender;
Hides within her bosom, too,
All her sorrows, bitter rue.

Light the green candle and place it among the plants, being careful not to scorch the leaves. Softly chant your charm or selected verse in order to add some drama to the occasion. Take a sip of water from the glass and pour the remainder into the plants with the words: *'With water from the well, I dedicate this sacred space to the spirit of the garden'*. Sit or stand for few moments and enjoy the peace and calm of your newly dedicated space.

Remember: A quiet corner prepared with loving care is the only sacred space you need, and if it's big enough to stand in, it's big enough to use magically.

Chapter Nine – Spiritual Transformation

Sooner or later, we have to return to the question of *what* witches believe. Even if we accept that true Craft is *not* a religion – because it's an individual's *natural ability* that distinguishes a witch – then does this mean that traditional witches have no religious affiliations?

Not at all. Back in the good old days, after most pagan agricultural festivals and celebrations had been absorbed into the Christian calendar, the local wise woman might even have been seen as a church-going, card-carrying member of the parish. This idea is borne out by the fact that, even today, traditional Craft persists in using the old Church calendar names for the major festivals that remained very much part of the agricultural year despite the repackaging:

- Candlemas: 2nd February - the Church festival of the purification of the Virgin Mary. Church-goers brought household candles for a blessing that was supposed to ward off evil in the home, but this practice was banned after the Reformation. Also the old Celtic festival of Imbolc and the start of the lambing season.

- Roodmas: 1st May – a commemoration of the finding of the true cross (OE *rod* = meaning cross or gallows) that can be documented back to the 900s: *rod* possibly referring to the crossed piece that the person is hung from on the gallows. There is also the triumph of the cross on 14th September. In Scotland and Ireland it was Beltaine, a pagan fire-festival marking the first day of summer when cattle were turned out to graze.

- Lammas: 1st August – an old feast day celebrating the first fruits of the harvest from OE *hlāf-mæsse* = loaf and feast. It was also the time when meadows were reopened for common grazing, marked by country fairs and other festivities. In Ireland and Scotland this day marked Lughnasadh, a festival to honour the pagan god of light and wisdom, with singing, dancing and merrymaking around evening bonfires.

- Hallowmas: 1st November – the feast of All Hallows or All Saints from OE *hālgian* = to hallow and *hālga* = saint. Although it was a joyous Christian religious festival, it also marks the eve of All Soul's Day when prayers were said for the dead. In Ireland and Scotland it was called Samhain, a pagan festival marking the transition between summer and winter. It began during the night of 31st October with bonfires and superstitious rituals, and was thought to be a time when supernatural activity was at its height. Hence giving rise to many of the customs and beliefs now associated with Hallowe'en.

Despite attempts to re-introduce the use of the Celtic names in the 1980s, genuine old Craft incantations still call on Christian saints, many of whom had strong pagan associations before being 'adopted' by the Church. This practice is considered to be an integral part of traditional witchcraft and widely quoted in popular books of the 1970s. [Similarly, the use of the Celtic seasonal names is still commonplace in Ireland, but not connected in any way to pagan belief.] This is also true of both the Romany and practitioners of voodoo/Santeria; both of whom have a strong magical culture that is performed under a thin veneer of Christian belief. The following are genuine 17th century examples of using Christian symbolism for rites of protection:

The Old Wives' Prayer

Holy-rood, come forth and shield
Us i' the city and in the field;
Safely guard us, now and aye,
From the blast that burns by day,
And those sounds that us afright
In the dead of dampish night:
Drive all hurtful fiends us from,
By the time the cocks first crow.

or

Charms

Bring the holy crust of bread,
Lay it underneath the head;
'Tis a certain charm to keep
Hags away while children sleep

An old-fashioned witch might not have had the enquiring mind or educational opportunities of her 21st century counterparts, but she would have had the advantage of absorbing teaching passed on within an oral tradition that had persisted for hundreds of years. Lacking in intellect but not in application, the witch of yesteryear would probably have fully understood the sentiments expressed in a collection of spiritual essays dating from 1897 [*The Treasure of the Humble*], wherein the author writes about *Ultima Thule* – the extreme limit – and which also can be applied to traditional Craft.

We are here on the 'borderland of human thought and far across the Artic circle of the spirit. There is no ordinary cold, no ordinary dark there, and yet you shall find there naught but flames and light. But to those who arrive without having trained their minds *to these new perceptions, the light and flames are as dark and cold as though they were painted. This means that the intelligence, the reason, will not suffice of themselves: we must have faith.*

It is not an easy matter to define faith, as opposed to religion. Perhaps we can begin by quoting from another 100-year-old essay on the subject: *"Religion is the effective desire to be in the right relation to the Power manifesting itself in the universe."* It will be seen that this definition has two implications, (1) the belief in the existence of a Power (or Powers) manifesting itself in the universe, and (2) the desire on the part of mankind to put itself into a right relationship to it. The first has in it the germ of *faith*, the second, religion.

This faith, which is considered by anthropologists to be more ancient than recognised religion, is an acceptance of the existence of supranormal forces that can influence or change the course of events. And the force (or energy) was thought of as residing either in natural objects, or in actions and words that are evoked to control these events. The witch has always had an unshakeable faith in the Way of the Wise, irrespective of the dominant religion of the time, and this may also be an indication of why witches were always viewed as standing outside the established church or community. They may have been dismissed as ignorant, cantankerous old women, but in some things they were infinitely wiser than those who persecuted them.

Nevertheless, the village witch (or wise woman) would have been regularly called upon to act as midwife, or to dispense herbal medicine for sickly children and animals. No doubt she would have flung the occasional curse about in order to relieve the boredom: and to maintain the fear and respect of her neighbours. This installation of fear also kept her safe, and free from interference from those who would perhaps persecute a woman living alone. If her neighbours felt uncomfortable in her presence, they could always keep her sweet (as the saying goes) by the giving of gifts, in the form of bread, eggs, vegetables, a chicken, etc., and keep their distance – until the next time they needed to call upon her skills.

We must also remember that the concept of witchcraft in Anglo-Saxon and Medieval England differed considerably from the hysteria that surrounded the later Tudor-Stuart 'burning times', and happenings in continental Europe. Up to around c1500, witchcraft was viewed as damage to crops or cattle livestock by spells or poison; or to people, ranging from sickness, sterility and death. *The crime was not considered serious* – it was a crime against a neighbour, rather than a crime against God – and the penalties tended to be like those for any other anti-social act. Conviction carried a relatively light punishment and few suffered death, unless they had caused the death of another human being. As late as 1467, by which time thousands of witches had been burned in France, a convicted diviner who was trying to help locate thieves by the means of scrying, merely had to appear in public with a scroll on his head!

The kernel of a traditional witch's faith, however, is a belief in a definite association of force (or energy) within special localities, and the notion of natural energy influencing cause and effect. The term 'animism' was first coined in the early 18th century by Georg Ernst Stahl to describe his philosophy of a world soul; the word *anima*, meaning 'breath', which in Latin came to have the secondary sense of 'soul' = breath of life. The belief embraces the notion that spirits [or natural energy] inhabit everything in Nature – every hill, tree and stream, every breeze and cloud, every stone and pool has its own 'spirit'. According some anthropologists, animism is the grass roots of all religion, and so the theory was consigned to the box of 'primitive thought' ... but it's the nearest we can come to understanding what presses the *spiritual* buttons of the traditional witch.

We should not, however, take this to mean that a traditional witch is spiritually backward. The most amazing thing for us to consider, is that all this wondrous insight into the metaphysical world would have been passed down via an intuitive oral tradition, amongst people with no (or little) formal learning. In reality, it *is* perfectly possible to perceive ourselves as a spiritual beings without being at all religious. Spirituality is how we 'feel' about the meaning of life – it is the quest for the hidden mysteries and need not manifest itself in religious terms.

Learning to explore different facets of spirituality also teaches us more about how to recognise that answers (from divination) are subjective to where an individual is standing *at the precise moment in time at which they pose the question.* Like magical correspondences, any revelation is unique to the individual, since there are no ground rules to govern how, when and where it is to be found. Again, we return to the importance of being able to recognise and understand the relevance of intuition and correspondence in the urban witch's world. There are few things in life that can be categorised into simple terms of black and white – the experienced witch comes to see the world in forty shades of grey. This does not mean indecision, or developing an eclectic frame of mind: in a spiritual context this means that there is certainly more than one pathway when it comes to following Craft teaching.

The witch's familiarity in dealing with natural spirit entities led to the accusations of trafficking with demons. One of the characteristics of animism, however, is that the spirits are *not* regarded, for the most part, as malignant, but rather as neutral or even amenable. This is borne out by the ritual of offering and supplication. Study any of the genuine spell books and in almost all cases it is not a grovelling attempt at the 'conciliation of capricious beings', who are seen as taking a perverse pleasure in inflicting harm and damage, but rather a sober and dignified approach to the appropriate spirit or entity.

The spirits (or *numina* as the Romans called them) are acknowledged as being powerful in their own individual spheres, and though regarded with respect, they are looked upon as being reasonable and ready to help if given their due. A witch asks that the spirits will be propitious in granting the request, and in return they are offered the witch's best. Obviously there is an element of placation in all this, but it is a free-will offering, which accepts that the spirits too, have their Will, and may grant the witch's request ... or not, as the case may be. A witch has the *right* to ask, but not necessarily to receive.

This faith in the natural world, however, should not be viewed as a worship of Nature. It is rather more a reverence *for* Nature in all her guises – and often red in tooth and claw when we enter the domain of living creatures.

Magical Ethics & Morality

Hundreds of years of adverse publicity has done little to dispel the myth that witches have little or no morality, but as we discussed in the first chapter of this book, traditional Craft is governed by *the personal morality of the individual.*

There is, however, a vast difference between magical ethics and magical morality. Ethics govern our dealings with fellow crafters and those turning to us for help. Morality is a personal yardstick. It is having the strength to undertake a magical working and then taking full responsibility for our actions. It is also accepting that what might be morally justifiable in one given set of circumstances, may not be quite so cut and dried in other situations. This is best summed up in that famous Qabalistic quote concerning misplaced force (or energy):

It can be misplaced in time: like the violence that is acceptable in war, in unacceptable in peace. It can be misplaced in space: like a burning coal on the rug rather than the fireplace. Or it can be misplaced in proportion: like an excess of love can make us overly sentimental, or a lack of love can make us cruel and destructive ...

The witch's viewpoint can often be seen as a conflicting standard of morality, simply because their mind is trained to see things from different perspectives. These differing viewpoints can be best illustrated by what are often referred to as the 'Seven Holy Virtues' – faith, hope, charity, prudence, justice, fortitude and temperance. On the surface we could say that these offer up a template for living a good life, but what happens if misplaced 'force' generates *excessive* virtue?

Faith: An over-zealous approach to faith can result in narrow-mindedness, bigotry and, at times, what is seen as a justified vicious persecution of those of other faiths or beliefs.

Hope: To put our trust in, or blindly have confidence in some future event, can seriously backfire if no effort is put into resolving matters of today. Relying solely on the outcome of future happenings to alter our situation may eventually lead to depression and stagnation when things don't according to plan.

Charity: Misplaced emphasis behind doing charitable deeds may be fuelling a personal 'feel-good' factor that enhances an individual in their own eyes, and turn out to be a monumental ego-trip of self-importance, rather than ay genuine desire to help the less fortunate.

Prudence: Whilst there is nothing wrong with being cautious and careful of the consequences of our actions, we may miss out on much of what life has to offer. By holding back to weigh up the pros and cons, others can take advantage and make off with the prize – which may leave us with a feeling of bitterness and resentment.

Justice: To use an old Buddhist adage: Justice without Mercy can be as counter-productive as Mercy without Justice. A sense of being overly just can descend into an outright cruelty, which can still function within the law.

Fortitude: A strength of mind that enables us to meet difficulty or endure pain without complaint can often produce negative responses in those around us. Being too self-contained may lead to abandonment or rejection by those close to us.

Temperance: Moderation and self-restraint, especially in the indulgence of the appetites and passions can greatly influence how we view the behaviour of others, making us judgemental and self-righteous.

A traditional witch doesn't set themselves up as a guardian of public sensibilities, neither do they feel the need to take responsibility for society's short-comings. This is not because the witch is cruel or unfeeling, it is just that they see things from a much broader viewpoint, including the sad reality that mankind causes much of its own misfortune. We may choose to help on a local, or personal level, but this is the decision of the individual, and not due to any social duty or obligation. In a nutshell … we merely look after our own.

Exercise:

We are now returning to the question raised in Chapter One: *Which path will you ultimately tread?* In following the various magical and meditation exercises, you will have started to become aware of the different levels of consciousness. To repeat Pamela Balls' advice, that we should always bear in mind that any changes that happen during magical or meditation working, initially take place on the *inner* planes of consciousness. These changes are far more subtle than those that affect us on the outer levels, and we may not be aware of them occurring until our perceptions on *both* levels begin to alter the way we look at things.

Let's start by trying to define your own personal image of the Creative Power, and how you see him/her/it in the grand scheme of things. Is the image of:

- A benign, patriarchal/matriarchal figure

- Being 'out there' and/or conversely 'in me'

- A divine creative force

There is nothing wrong in needing anthropomorphism [*Chambers Dictionary: the conception of a god as having the form, personality or attributes of a human being; ascription of human characteristics to what is not human.*] to help us focus on what is otherwise an abstract idea of spiritual force. As Professor Bailey observes in *Phases in the Religion of Ancient Rome*, it was difficult enough for early people to understand – it remains difficult for modern, sophisticated people – to conceive of an identity apart from human identity.

Unfortunately, this is where the edges get blurred between faith and religion, and it is at this level we find classic deities morphing into the modern pagan pantheon, regardless of their origins or function. All gods and goddesses have become one ... but still with a very distinct *human* form. The spirit of the place has developed functions beyond mere guardianship of a specific 'place' and attained much a wider significance; a process of change from spirit of place to god(dess) of *function*. Meditate on this imagery as represented in the Tarot in the form of **the Empress** (a beneficent Queen and the epitome of charity and kindness); and **the Emperor** (a great King, a wise and powerful ruler: all that is positive in the masculine persona).

The vague idea of 'something' being out there and/or conversely in ourselves denotes the we have attained a certain level of spiritual transformation, but are reluctant to distance ourselves from the belief that we are somehow an important item in the scheme of things. We still have a foot in both camps, so to speak, but the intangible 'something' is an idea that is poking around in our subconscious. From your Tarot pack select the images of **the Priestess** (a Wise Woman who instructs in the art of occult knowledge) and **the Hierophant** (a Teacher who imparts esoteric knowledge to the people in a practical and oral way they can understand). We should also reflect on how these two cards of the major arcana flank those of the Empress and the Emperor.

Witches of old, of course, were simple souls, and although they intuitively understood the basic machinations behind Craft working, they also knew it gave the spell-casting added *oomph* if some sort of super-force were invoked! The old Craft appellation for this energy is the Old Lass and the Old Lad, a kind of verbal magical shorthand that speaks volumes in simple country terms of endearment. Animism has in it the *element* of true religion for it is a recognition of higher powers and of man's dependence on them, but it is possessed of a realisation of the immense spiritual power *behind* the veil of the Priestess = the true meaning of life. The two Tarot cards that represent this aspect of faith are **the Devil** (the card often referred to as Pan and the force of unbridled Nature) and **the Star** (the symbol of timeless Mystery and the ever-turning cosmos).

Important note: Whatever impressions you receive from this exercise, they won't be the same for you as it is for me; neither will your experience match the sensations felt by other readers of this book. Only you can interpret the 'signs'.

For the urban witch (for it is s/he who is the principal player in this unfolding drama) there is great scope for exploring the Way of the Wise. For especially in the towns and cities, there are sacred pagan sites and locations that have remained unpolluted by urban development. When Pope Gregory sent St Augustine to convert the Anglo-Saxons in the 6th century he told him: "Do not pull down the *fanes* (temples) ... purify [them] with holy water, set relics there and let them become temples of the true God. So the people will have no need to change their place of concourse, and where of old they were wont to sacrifice ... thither let them continue to resort on the day of the saint to whom the Church is dedicated ... in honour of Him whom they now worship."

Let's employ a little bit of reverse psychology here. One of the most enduring features in the whole history of religion, is the way in which people have clung to the sacred places of their far-off ancestors. The 'invaders' gained prestige by occupying a holy site, overthrowing the old religion and replacing it with new ritual observance. Sacred trees, springs and stones were also incorporated into the construction of churches and churchyards, with pagan and Christian symbols mingling freely amongst the architectural carvings.

I suggested earlier in the book that one of the most effective places for peace and meditation for the urban witch, is often a local church, especially if its foundations are very old. There are more than 230 remaining churches that are basically (or in part) Anglo-Saxon – built between the 7th century and the Norman Conquest. The parish will be proud of its ancient history, so there will be no difficulty in establishing the building's antecedents. Remember that most of these small churches would have originally been built in village locations, before the urban sprawl swallowed them up, and the hallowed pagan aura here is probably less polluted than at the majestic crowd-pullers of Avebury and Stonehenge!

Among natural objects, which have always been regarded

with reverence, was the spring – and there is no spring that is not sacred – with the old animistic notion of its spirit surviving throughout our long history. The basic requirement for these so-called 'holy wells' is that the water should still flow, bubble, or 'well' up from the ground (OE *wella, wiella*) so as to maintain the eternal fascination we feel towards the life-giving spring. Our pagan ancestors threw offerings into the water (many of which have been recovered during excavations) in return for healing or prophesy.

Again, the Church authorities realised that these customs were fundamental impulses better 'redirected than repressed'. In order to circumnavigate the continued belief in the curative power of the spirit of the spring, a saint was assigned to the 'well' and the offering to the spirit became a thanks-gift to the Church. By the medieval period, the 'holy wells' had become lucrative curative centres; modern well-dressing ceremonies are a revival and extension of these old beliefs, though the theme is usually an illustration from the Bible. Every town and city will have countless 'well' streets and all it takes is an hour or two spent in the local library to enable you to locate your nearest sacred spring.

Groves and trees too, were thought of as the habitation of spirits, both recorded as being sacred to the Druids and Iceni. Yew trees, in particular – some believed to be up to 1000-years old – are still to be found in old churchyards, and if they are more than 1000-years old, they may well have marked sites of pagan worship prior to the arrival of Christianity. According to tree expert, John Moore, those trees found on religious sites usually *do* pre-date the current theological use, and are often older than the existing buildings.

The early Church calendar, as we know, was founded on the pagan agricultural year and by the late medieval period [c1400-1580] the building would have been the village community's usual gathering place. Young men went to church to survey the young women, with one attempted seduction even taking place during evensong! The relation of the Church to the turning points of the year – Christmas and the Winter Solstice, Easter and the Spring Equinox – meant that many pre-Christian observances could readily be accommodated within the religious framework. These patently pagan observances were absorbed into the religious calendar *and remain there to this day*.

There is, however, precedence for town-folk being encouraged to participate in rural revels. In ancient Rome, festivals to mark the sowing and the harvest were observed in both urban and rural celebrations, with cattle and men jumping through blazing bonfires. This wasn't just an excuse for merry-making, but because the towns and cities needed provisions through the winter months, it was necessary for the correct rituals to be carried out to ensure the continuous supply of food for the urban populace.

The outcome of all this was the close interweaving of two separate sets of belief, much of which *had little to do with the actual Christian year*. So, for the urban witch, a quiet contemplation in an old church, under an old yew tree in the corner of a churchyard, or by a 'holy well', should not be considered a breaking of the faith, or compromising our integrity. Even the Church calendar marks the turning of the pagan year ... we are merely reclaiming our own.

Chapter Ten – Moving on …

Much of what we have discussed so far has led us towards introducing a sense of peace and tranquillity *'even in the city's throng'*, whereby we can learn to switch off from the noise and hubbub that is constantly going on around us, **in order to develop our Craft abilities**. Noise can be defined as 'unwanted sound' and while we all have different tolerance levels, once that level is breeched, it produces stress. Peace and tranquillity, however, doesn't mean wrapping ourselves in a cocoon of total silence, but being able to mentally induce a state of stillness, serenity and calm at Will.

As urban witches, we need to develop this art of freeing ourselves from distractions and worries, albeit temporarily, and allow the magical side of our nature to take flight.

We accept that the environment in which we live is not always conducive to successful magical working due the constant barrage of negative energy that we confront on a daily basis, but we are beginning to *learn to live life how we choose*. It's possible that we've already made some alterations to our home environment in order to accommodate this new-found 'freedom', but we know there isn't a simple seven-point plan we can implement by picking up a book and following the instructions.

Hopefully, by now we will have introduced a modicum of detachment into our lives, because we've spent a lot of time developing the *right* environment in which we can progress magically. We have probably also started to change our basic attitude to the way we look at things and behave, because an urban witch's circumstances often differ quite considerably from our Wiccan counterparts. We accept that we may not be able to change our external circumstances but we *can* change our attitude to the way we approach problems and difficulties.

Exercise:

Trying to live a magical existence requires some personal space in which we can reflect upon the changes that are being brought about in ourselves by the close proximity to psychic energy we are now generating on a regular basis. This can be thought of in terms of a private space where we can just 'be'. If our green space isn't adequate (a kitchen window sill or front garden, for example), then it can be any part of the house or flat where we can snatch a few moments; even behind the closed door of the bathroom while relaxing in a soothing bath.

One of my students (another urban witch), who had spent many years studying yoga, gave me this exercise, which she uses to create a buffer between 'everyday stuff and magic time'. There are times, of course, when we need to throw a bit of magical weight around on the spur of the moment but, in most cases, we're better off creating our own psychological barrier to help us switch off. Creating a pleasant atmosphere helps relaxation and clears the mind before casting our Circle.

Angie's relaxation technique:

"This simple exercise is usually done to 'earth' yourself after a yoga sequence, but it can be used at anytime during the day when there is 10 minutes to spare. It is best performed lying flat on the floor, legs slightly apart and feet flopped to the sides. Arms should be to the side, with hands relaxed, so that you can visualise the body slowly sinking into the ground. Eyes can be open or closed.

"We are not attempting to push any thoughts away, but allowing them to float across the mind like a TV screen with the sound turned off. This is not a time for sorting out problems, so there is no need to concentrate on holding any particular mental image – just let things drift. Try not to fall asleep but if you do, no harm is done because there are no 'energy points' open. The exercise is also useful for anyone who finds it difficult to sleep at night. When you feel calm, gently raise your hands above your head and sit up slowly. Now you are ready to begin your magical preparation ..."

NB: I include this exercise to show that the teacher can always learn something from a student.
"Who is the teacher and who is the taught? You think you're the seeker and find you're the sought."

Once an old-time traditional witch had been instructed in the 'Way of the Wise' she would probably have been content with her lot, and never considered moving away from her village. Through trial and error, she would have expanded her knowledge of wort-lore, and become more efficient in honing other magical skills, but there would have been no personal pressure to push the boundaries of esoteric knowledge on a more intellectual level. Today's urban witch doesn't have the luxury of being content merely to 'be' ... the pagan community now has so much access to information that it can often produce a feeling of dissatisfaction or boredom within the simple confines of Craft.

Much of what we learn about alternative beliefs and practices as embraced by the celebrity A-List, are to be found on the Internet, or in women's magazines and weekend colour supplements. Who hasn't read about the sexual prowess of one celeb endorsing Tantra? Or learned the secrets of the latest exponent of *ayurveda*, an ancient Indian medicine; or Qabalistic mysticism? Or Ashtanga yoga? Or the faith-healer, whose clientele includes an impressive line-up of celebrities and politicians? Not to mention aromatherapy, sweat lodges, dream quests, chakra healing, *Tai Chi, reiki, feng shui*, I-Ching and colour therapy, to name but a few.

Often these practices are packaged in such a way that they appear glamorous or other-worldly – we're attracted to them by their very 'exoticness'. We pick up the glossy magazines and find ourselves bombarded by articles extolling the virtues of holistic healing and herbalism. Nearly every major celebrity appears to have a personal guru (whose fees run into megabucks), instructing him or her in the latest fad ... that involves drinking a 'soul-boosting mixture of body fluids'. We know that one celeb favours colonic irrigation; while another drinks a potion of milk mixed with their own urine as part of their spiritual development.

Unfortunately, the glamour and mystery of the different and new has a strong influence over the gullible high-street shopper, who falls for the sales patter and come away convinced that a very expensive crystal really *will* enhance their spirituality. The urban witch needs a healthy degree of scepticism and discernment, because many of the so-called experts only have a weekend workshop between them ... and within a few weeks they have become teachers, recommending books and therapies left, right and centre. No wonder good, old-fashioned traditional witchcraft can often feel tame by comparison!

Because we become desperate for more magical sensation, it is easy to become tempted by those who claim to be able to help us along the Way – if only we'll just step down this side road. We *want* to believe; we *want* to experience – and we're willing to follow anyone who promises to show us how. At this point, many a newcomer gets lost in a series of one-way systems and blind alleys to such a degree that they either settle for second best, or give up altogether. This is where we find would-be witches falling into several different categories.

- Those looking for someone who will tell them what to do, and who will often latch on to a flamboyant group leader with a high degree of inflated self-importance. They fall for the dressing up and psycho-drama rather than any serious conviction as to the antecedents of their new guru.

- Those who seize upon anything that's new in order to be different amongst their own social set. They 'play' for a while and then follow the next new fad because they don't want to put in the hard work necessary to develop any measure of knowledge: just enough to keep them ahead of the rest.

- Those who are desperately seeking that unidentifiable *something* to fill a void in their lives. Often they are looking for a new set of rules to apply to their daily routine, and will experiment with other cultures that appear attractive to them. Their 'belief' becomes an eclectic blend of Eastern and Western techniques, embracing everything from the strongholds of the Tibetan lama to the wide plains of the North American shaman.

- Those who will embrace a tradition on a physical or superficial level, because they want the recognition and rank without putting in the effort to acquire genuine understanding. They will often try to make themselves indispensable to a well-known figure within that tradition.

- Those who from the first introduction know that this is what they've always wanted. This is what they *are*. They no longer need to look for the Way; the Way has found them. *They have become the Way.*

Regardless of any Craft teaching we decide to take on board, it is impossible to go very far without coming up against the exhortation: 'Know Thyself!' With the best will in the world, trying to reflect constructively upon the positive and negative traits to our character is like looking into a watery mirror. The reflection is there but the lines are blurred and distorted – while the slightest ripple can shatter the image completely. The watery mirror also conceals that which we don't want to see, or that which remains out of reach. At this stage of our Craft learning we still need to put things into proper perspective and accept that we are trying to define something intangible in tangible terms. It will be some time before we can emulate Jung and say: *"I don't believe! I know!"*

Crossing the Dark River

The famous 'dark night of the soul' is not a myth, as many who have undergone the experience will testify, and anyone with a genuine desire to understand true Craft will, sooner or later, need to cross that dark river. It symbolises a transition from one psychic state, or level of consciousness, to another; and crossing the boundary marks another milestone in our magical lives. It is also a state of mind often characterised by depression, disbelief, uncertainty and a feeling of personal unworthiness. The experience tends to arise immediately before a breakthrough to fresh understanding.

It may be a different perspective on the way we look at things – or it may be a strange and unfamiliar hand that beckons. We have to accept that any change on either the inner personality, or the outer actions *do* and *will* affect those with whom we share our lives and beliefs. When we set out to discover true Craft, we were probably tempted to talk about it because we wanted to share the excitement and the adventure. Be assured, very few will share your enthusiasm for many reasons.

A friend, who is also a psychotherapist describes it as being a time when the witch takes the traditional 'leap into the void' – "Where one lets go of all safety harnesses of training, text books, supervisors, and other people's approval and says: *It is so!* Once that moment has been achieved, one has a new perspective on Life, the Universe and Everything." This means we have to seriously re-consider or re-valuate just what it is that we think we believe in.

There is, of course, a price to be paid. For the newly-aware witch, especially one who belongs to a formal group, will have to put up with the disapproval of fellow pagans, who do not understand what has brought about these changes. It's almost as if the familiar circle of people, jobs, interests, social group, etc., has become too small and restricting to contain us any longer. "We have to cross its boundary into a larger (more inclusive) world and it's unlikely few (if any) of our friends will want to come with us," my tame psychotherapist warned. "They may well try to stop us leaving, argue that we are 'wrong'. We have to choose – stay and suffocate, or to go on and be lonely, scared, clumsy, unknowing. Sooner or later we choose to move on."

What we need to realise is that none of these problems are uncommon. As the psychotherapist says, we may need to examine the beneath-the-surface assumptions of the circles in which we move, and ask ourselves whether we agree with what is expected of us. If we no longer agree with them, or do not wish to live up to those expectations, or feel that we have outgrown the present situation, then we will never be satisfied or fulfilled while we remain within those restrictions. The choice of where we want to go next is ours – *and ours alone*.

Under these circumstances, the urban witch may find it almost impossible to simply 'move on' because of the overspill of close social, emotional and mental pressures that materialise to prevent us from striking out on our own. We may even find that we come up against open hostility and resentment from those with whom we've shared the Circle. This is the time of the 'dark night of the soul' when doubt and fear invade the psyche and put *faith* to the test. At this time, *to thine own self be true* and, by adopting an inner honesty about yourself and your own abilities, you will discover that honest self-appraisal can be a powerful weapon against self-doubt and low self-esteem.

Let's stand back and reflect for a moment on how far we've come:

We began with a gentle **learning** curve that acknowledged the unique problems faced by an urban witch. Despite the numerous magazine articles, books and courses on the subject, however, we now know that personal Craft development is not a commodity that can be acquired with a credit card and a couple of weekend workshops, since access to information does not automatically bring instant understanding. This is in stark contrast to the proliferation of 'quick-fix' self-help techniques that have become so popular in recent years.

The next step was to develop our **conviction** that we *could* do something about improving our own magical environment – but not by drawing on information from any source without checking its authenticity. While there are hundred of books in the mind, body & spirit genre written by 'nice' people, whose view of witchcraft is 'nice', it does not mean that they have lived the Craft they publish.

With growing **determination**, we learned how to overcome the barriers to successful Craft working within a recognisably hostile environment. Once we began to take control, we began to feel the courage of our convictions pushing us forward with a strange sense of determination to succeed, by increasing our awareness of what we *can* achieve. By this stage we will have come to realise that we cannot actively work towards our own Craft identity by reading books and remaining as a casual observer. The time for play-acting is over and the time has come for assuming responsibility for our future actions.

Transforming determination into **action** moves our learning from the 'if-only' into the realms of practical, hands-on magic. This is our 'coming out' whereby we begin to live our life under a new set of rules and our magical awareness plumbs new depths. We are no longer afraid of pushing the boundaries and experiencing new sensations, because we understand how and why we need to maintain the high level of protection from the negativity that will always be a peripheral problem for an urban witch.

Only sustained **effort** can implement the actual changes. These changes must become a permanent way of life in order to overcome any form of negative residue from our previous situation. It is important, however, to accept that these inner changes will not take place overnight, our new-found Craft identity needs time to acquire its own habit or pattern. As with all things, magical success will only come in proportion to the amount of effort put into the preparation.

It is also important to realise that unless the changes we hope to bring about are spontaneous, and automatically become part of our daily life, then the **transformation** is incomplete. Going through the motions is not enough since this merely results in the growth of self-importance rather than self-esteem. By gaining self-understanding we inspire confidence within ourselves; and a healthy sense of self-confidence is a critical factor in achieving our goals.

Shades and Shadows

In Chapter One we casually mentioned the comfortable familiarity that all witches should have with the spirits of the dead, and asked how comfortable you were with the close proximity to the supernatural world.

The term 'Otherworld' can have alarming connotations to those unfamiliar with the concept. We are not just talking about those *ghoulies and ghosties, and long-legged beasties, and things that go bump in the night*. We are also referring to those inexplicable natural occurrences such as spontaneous lucid dreaming, co-incidences and *déjà vu* – which we've all experienced to a greater or lesser degree during our lives. Who hasn't found themselves confused, intrigued or disconcerted by any of these happenings

– or the involuntary shiver *'when someone walks over your grave'*? We ponder and reflect for a moment and then forget about it until the next time.

Many things happen on the periphery of our 'vision' – occurrences that are so fleeting that it's only with hindsight, or when someone else talks about a similar experience, that we remember them. Under normal circumstances, the lack of an acceptable explanation or interpretation discourages us from exploring further even if it leaves as residue of puzzlement in our mind. The exploration of Craft leads to the discovery of these 'gateways between the worlds' or different levels of consciousness, and makes us more aware of the open channels between these strange experiences.

If witches talk of something as being 'otherworldly' we are referring to those ethereal qualities summed up by the dictionary definition as: *'resembling celestial ether, light, airy, tenuous, subtle, exquisite, impalpable, spiritual'.* We can often catch these sensations at dusk and dawn when natural light take on an 'otherworldly' quality – casting a translucent sheen over the city-scape – changing plain, red-brick buildings into glowing terracotta temples, with grimy windows transformed into sparkling pools of light. If we stop and enjoy the moment, we're left with a feeling of exhilaration and vitality that can take several hours to evaporate; and then we wonder why we allowed ourselves to be so moved by that which is normal daily occurrence.

Then the moment is gone – until next time when we connect with our environment for a few precious moments. Although these experiences are fleeting, we harbour no doubts as to the reality of the sensation. We are being introduced to a totally new and different form of consciousness, which we will find almost impossible to describe to those who have not shared a similar experience. This is where we often begin to separate from our family and friends, who no longer understand the direction in which we are heading.

These glimpses of Otherworld are but an introduction and preparation for the deeper realms of Craft mysteries. The real witch *can* summon the spirits of our ancestors (or what we may look upon as our 'guardians'), and have the skill to call upon those entities that inhabit the 'between worlds' to do our bidding. A real witch *can* and *will* curse, but rarely does, simply because of the sustained effort required to carry a successful curse through to its logical conclusion is rarely worth the time and trouble. Finally, a real witch must be able to *find a way* through the maze encountered during a transformational experience that all within Craft must face and, should it be necessary, to descend into Otherworld to *accompany the dead* on their final journey.

It may seem strange to mention the importance of the hearth-fire in the next breath, but there *is* a very important otherworld-ancestral connection between the two. From the time the hearth was first placed at the centre of the house beneath an opening in the roof, it provided the centre of warmth and sustenance for the household. The hearth was in the charge of the women of the household, whose duty it was always to keep the fire alive, for in the primitive family it would be a serious matter if the fire went out.

From both Iron and Bronze-Age excavations, it would appear that it was also customary to bury the bodies of relatives beneath the house. These were not simply older burials over which houses had been accidentally built: the bodies had deliberately been placed there. When those from a Bronze Age site were sent for routine carbon 14 dating, it was discovered that the male had already been dead for 600 years when he was buried, and his female companion had only been dead for 300 years when she was re-interred!

The re-burials of these long-dead ancestors beneath a family home suggests that the simple notion of the ancestor of the hearth-fire developed into the concept of a collective guardian of the house, a benevolent spirit who watched over the fortunes of the family from generation to generation. For Craft purposes the sacred flame of the hearth-fire is, of course, the most obvious focus, for witches require no formal temples or sanctuaries – theirs was the magic of the hearth and bound to the spirit of the ancestors who continued to protect when called upon. Later superstitions of protective human skulls kept in a house (which were believed to cause havoc if anyone tried to remove it from the premises), may be a throw-back to this prehistoric link of ancestral belief.

Magic of the hearth-fire (or domestic magic) remains the province of the traditional witch and again, there are numerous recorded customs and superstitions emanating from it, although these may vary from different locations around the country. *The Penguin Guide to the Superstitions of Britain & Ireland* has stripped away the murkiness surrounding Victorian folk-lore 'niceties' and offers some tantalising glimpses of superstitious practices, which no doubt passed for magic in the old days! The urban witch may no longer have the luxury of an open fire in the home, but in our hearts there still burns the sacred flame of the hearth.

Nevertheless, here we have a glimpse into the existence of the Mysteries within true Craft, but there is no point in looking for any published material on the subject, because it does not exist. The Mysteries are there ... but they can only be fully understood through personal dedication and experience. Neither is there a Master at whose feet we can sit, and drink in the wisdom of his (or her) words. There's an old adage in esoteric circles that we will discover our next teacher when we are ready to receive the wisdom they are willing to bestow on us. *"When the pupil is ready, the Master appears"*. This means that the student must advance by his or her own efforts, before they need – or have 'earned' – the physical presence of a teacher: in whatever guise they may appear.

Sounds: Near and Far

There is nothing wrong in seeking to broaden the mind in esoteric matters, but it must be for the right reasons. If we wish to explore other paths and traditions, other than that in which we began, we must be truthful to ourselves when it comes to motive. Let's ask ourselves the following questions. Do we feel that we:

☐ Have come as far as we can at our present level of learning?

☐ Have become bored with the familiar?

☐ Not progressing quickly enough?

☐ Having difficulty in getting our magic to work?

☐ Have come as far as we want to go at the present time and require outside stimulus?

☒ If we feel we have come as far as we can at our present level of learning, then we need to go back to the drawing board and start again! Are we saying that for all the snippets of information, subtleties and direction about traditional Craft, *nothing* sparked our interest enough to want to find out more about things that haven't been included in our instruction to date? Perhaps we *still* think that we can find out all we require from books or weekend workshops, and don't need to explore further in order to transmute knowledge into understanding.

In Chapter One we asked the question: *Which path will you ultimately tread?* The answer is possibly that we need to accept traditional Craft isn't for us, and that we would be happier with one of the more eclectic pagan traditions offering something more varied.

☑ It's easy to become bored with familiar exercises and routines, especially if the results are slow in coming and we're working alone. As we've already discussed, Craft is a *natural ability* but as with all natural talents, some people still attain a level of competence much faster than others. What we need to do, is to find out whether our boredom stems from disinterest or frustration.

So, let's give ourselves a break and inject a little bit of 'displacement activity' into our routine. Displacement activity encompasses those things we find to do in order to put off a more important chore, but this time we can do it with a clear conscience. The following is a list of things to take time out to do:

- Visit the local museum or art gallery, and reflect on the religious art (ancient and modern) in the collection.

- Read at least one book on the mysticism of one of the major religions.

- Visit at least one sacred site (ancient or modern), and view it with an open mind and heart.

- Visit at least one natural beauty spot for the purpose of meditation and reflection.

In reality, these are just simple exercises to stimulate the mental juices and get things going again, just like a writer would do if suffering from 'writer's block'.

☑ It can be frustrating if we feel we're not progressing quickly enough but let's step back and have a look at our 'study' methods. As we've said before, *ten minutes practice a day is better than one hour once a week*. Or are we failing to create a barrier between 'workaday' stuff and magical exercise? Without the correct preparation, our channels won't be functioning properly, especially if we are tired or off-colour.

If lack of time is the problem, begin your preparation at home from the moment you walk in the door, because creating a pleasant atmosphere helps relaxation and soothes the mind. It doesn't matter if no magical exercises are incorporated to start with ... but get into the habit of doing the following:

- Set the radio on a timer so there is music playing when you walk in the door

- Change over to your favourite music on CD

- Make a refreshing cup of tea, or pour a glass of white wine

- Light a perfumed candle, evaporator or joss stick

- Run a deep bath with essential oils

- Relax for 20 minutes with tea or wine

- Soak in the bath for as long a possible

- Change into comfortable clothes

- Prepare a simple supper

- Relax with a book, or watch something interesting on TV

There's possibly nothing here that you don't do already. We are attempting to get you into a relaxed routine whereby a magical exercise slots in quite naturally at some stage, without becoming a chore.

☑ Perhaps we are becoming dispirited about having difficulty in getting our magic to work, but at least we are honest enough to admit it. *Knowing our abilities* and capabilities can save a lot of heartache and disappointment later on. Accept the fact that not everyone who *wants* to be a witch, was born with the inner ability to wield the magic of the Wise. Even excellent tuition from the best teacher available cannot bring out what was never there in the first place.

Again, the answer is possibly that we need to accept traditional Craft isn't for us, and that we would be happier with something more observational, rather than magical. Use the knowledge you have gained so far to find another path or tradition that isn't so demanding on the magical front. Many of the pagan groups are an eclectic blend of reconstructed European and Mediterranean folklore (which is best described as pantheistic), with a dash of Eastern promise. The beliefs are predominately Nature orientated (as opposed to agricultural), and there is an active social calendar for the pagan community in most large towns and cities.

☑ *'All work and no play ...'* We've come as far as we *want* to go at the present time and require some outside stimulus, in order to take a break from Craft studies. This is probably because we've taken it all so seriously that we've not given ourselves time to enjoy the trip. In other words: burn out – and it happens to the best! However we wish to define magic (and there are many ways), we have to face the fact that it is a very exhausting business. And if we've been highly successful in producing some impressive results on both the inner and outer planes, generating all this highly-charged energy *will* take its toll.

The advantage of being a town (or city)-based witch is that we have unlimited access to a huge information bank in the form of libraries, esoteric bookshops and 'new age' shops. Here we can find a whole range of different subjects that are still pertinent to our own individual area of study – including health and well-being, many forms of therapy and self-help, the practice of most esoteric or spiritual traditions, humanity and the environment. Find a topic and read about it for simple enjoyment. At the same time as broadening our awareness of other systems or cultures, it is also a reminder that the more we learn about magic ... the more we realise how *little* we actually know. Learn to take your foot off the pedal!

As the genie remarks in *Where The Rainbow Ends*, "Time is short and we have far to travel." Whilst it is always interesting to study and absorb information from other paths, traditions and cultures, we should never make the mistake of trying to incorporate them into our Craft working. In reality, traditional witchcraft has little formal history, but it is as old as time, and the grass roots from where all other belief systems sprang. To understand magic, however, we also need to be able to go back along the chain of civilisation and belief.

Throughout *Traditional Witchcraft for Urban Living* we have discussed the importance of understanding the natural (negative) energies from which the urban witch, in particular, might find themselves under attack, if the correct protective measures are not set firmly in place prior to Circle working. Even natural energy can be destructive if we haven't bothered to find out exactly *what* it is that we're channelling – and *all* of it should be looked upon as dangerous, if anyone believes they can control something they aren't even on nodding acquaintance with!

If we decided to magically explore other systems, then for reasons of self-protection we must learn to differentiate between the individual energies represented, for example, by Aphrodite (Greek), Venus (Roman), Hathor (Egyptian) Ishtar (Babylonian), Astarte (Phoenician) and Bridgit (Celtic). In modern, eclectic paganism, all these energies would be identified as having one source, i.e. the Goddess. To understand the power emanating from each source, however, we have to understand *what those ancient indigenous peoples who worshipped them called upon*, not what we read in contemporary quasi-magical books. If we read genuine magical texts, we are bombarded by classical references; all carefully controlled and contrived in order to convey *precise* information about the energy to be invoked.

When in doubt, I always refer to the *Encyclopaedia Britannica* because the information is based on scholarly research and not biased psuedo-esoteric writing. We may be surprised to learn that myth, folk-lore and legend (upon which much of Craft lore is based), is now recognised as a vital part of the development of the human race. It is also accepted that the roots of mythology and legend "is a kind of serious philosophy that was not random and which has its own peculiar logic, even if it is not rationalistic logic that sits comfortably within the remit of modern society." For as we discussed before, it is also necessary for the witch to wade through the irritating maze of analogies, allegories and symbols – all of which means making connections between things that outwardly and rationally aren't connected at all!

Going back to our anthropomorphic discussions in the last chapter, it is also important to accept that 'names' do not represent *real* people when calling upon deities, saints, entities, demons or spirits. It is wishful thinking to believe that God/dess is sitting there just waiting for our call: it is detrimental to genuine Craft thinking, too. In magic, we use these 'mind pictures' to invoke (or evoke) the *conceptualised* power of those individual energy sources, not the entities themselves.

Imagine for a moment that we are faced by a huge bank of colour-coded, electrical sockets, all having different strengths of electrical current running through them. These represent the source of magical energy we wish to harness for a particular spell. In our hands we have a selection of colour-coded plugs representing the nature of the magical working we wish to perform. If we make the wrong choice and connect the red plug to, say, a blue socket, it could result in a) insufficient current coming through to power the magical working, or b) over-load, in which case we blow a fuse and the whole working is either negated or incinerated.

This is why any magical practitioner *must* work through that irritating maze of correspondences. Because for successful magical results, it *does* mean making connections between signs and symbols which, outwardly and rationally, are not connected at all. It may also make it clear as to why we need to plug in to the right connection if we want to get our magic to work.

Natural ability or Illusion?

There *will* come a time when all witches ask themselves whether what they are experiencing is real, or just wishful thinking. There is nothing wrong in wanting proof, but unfortunately there are no prescribed rules governing what is, after all, a natural psychic ability. So let's look at the illusion, which appears to satisfy a large number of people who will sit and meditate or visualise for hours on end, and come out with nothing but a 'feel good factor'. There is nothing wrong with this either – but if that's all our magic does for us, we are kidding ourselves if we think *this* is Craft.

Set a dozen students a series of pathworkings and well over half will respond with the feeling of calm/relaxed/familiar/ warm/comforting/welcoming/etc., but as a highly accomplished witch once retorted in exasperation: "If you ain't scared shitless, you ain't doing it right!" And that just about sums it up. It doesn't matter how experienced we are, if there isn't that frisson of fear lurking around the periphery of the Circle, or the icy finger up the spine when we're magically engaged, then we are *not* on our contacts – we're just playing at it and all the psychodrama in the world isn't going to produce the results.

By questioning ourselves, we will also be questioning the claims of others, because we are not afraid of challenging 'the Emperor's New Clothes' syndrome, often encountered in pagan groups. They may claim to see all manner of textbook manifestations but you probably 'see' things on a different level. There has been a lot written about colours associated with the aura or other magical appearances but more often that not a student will be honest enough to admit that they don't register actual colour, and are often concerned that the absence of the spectrum within their workings means they aren't doing things right. You, however, may not be able to see a person's aura defined by colour, but you may be highly conscious of the energy field surrounding or emitting from that person.

Experienced witches don't work at textbook level and their inner senses may register things differently from non-magical, or ordinary pagan folk. Much of traditional Craft is intuitive, and the only thing that separates ability and illusion in the beginning is the physical results of a spell or charm. As the years go by, and the witch learns to hone those talents through repeated experience, the inner questioning of his or her own ability is no longer necessary ... **you'll know what you are.**

When one looks at it, one cannot see it:
When one listens for it, one cannot hear it:
When one seeks it, one cannot find it;
When one uses it, it is inexhaustible.

Here endeth the lesson ...

Source & Bibliography

The Aquarian Guide to the New Age, Eileen Campbell & J H Brennan (Aquarian)

Book of Diving the Future, Eva Shaw (Wordsworth)

The Book of Fortune Telling, Madame Fabia (Daily Express)

British Folk Customs, Christina Hole (Hutchinson)

Brother Cadfael's Herb Garden, Talbot & Whiteman (Little Brown)

The Complete Magic Primer, David Conway (Aquarian)

Countryside, Geoffrey Grigson (Ebury)

Culpeper's Coloured Herbal, Ed. David Potterton (Foulsham)

Culpeper's Complete Herbal (Wordsworth)

Culpeper's Medicine, Graeme Tobyn (Element)

The Curious Lore of Precious Stones, George Frederick Kunz (Dover)

Earth, Air, Fire Water, Skelton and Blackwood (Arkana)

The Encyclopaedia of Witchcraft & Demonology, Rossell Hope Robbins (Newnes)

Exploring Spirituality, Suzanne Ruthven & Aeron Medbh-Mara (How-To Books)

Fauna Britannica, Stefan Buczacki (Hamlyn)

Folklore, Myths & Legends of Britain (Reader's Digest)

Four Elements, Rebecca Rupp (Profile Books)

Green Magic, Lesley Gordon (Ebury Press)

Green Pharmacy, Barbara Griggs (Norman & Hobhouse)

Hesperides, Robert Herrick (Morely)

The Hollow Tree, Mélusine Draco (ignotus)

Magical Jewels of the Middle Ages and the Renaissance, Joan Evans (Dover)

Malleus Satani, Suzanne Ruthven (ignotus)

Memory, Wisdom & Healing, Gabrielle Hatfield (Sutton)

Natural Remedies (Readers' Digest)

Nature's Medicine Chest (Readers' Digest)

The Observer's Book of Old English Churches, Lawrence E Jones (Warne)

The Observer's Book of Pond Life, John Clegg (Warne)

Old Time Herbs for Northern Gardens, Minnie Watson Kamm (Dover)

The Pageant of England, Thomas B. Costain (Wyndham)

The Penguin Guide to the Superstitions of Britain & Ireland, Steve Roud (Penguin)

Perfume Power, Joules Taylor (London House)

Phases in the Religion of Ancient Rome, Prof Cyril Bailey (OUP)

RHS Encyclopaedia of Herbs & Their Uses, Deni Brown (RHS)

RHS Really Small Gardens, Jill Billington (RHS)

Root & Branch: British Magical Tree Lore, Draco and Harriss (ignotus)

Secret Wisdom, David Conway (Aquarian)

Seven Ages of Britain, Justin Pollard (Hodder & Stoughton)

The Sociology of Health & Healing, Margeret Stacey (Routledge)

Spells & Charms, Trish MacGregor (D&C)

Spells, Charms, Talismans & Amulets, Pamela Ball (Arcturus)

The Unofficial Countryside, Richard Mabey (Collins)

Vinegar: Nature's Secret Weapon, Maxwell Stein (Blackwell)

White Horse: Equine Magical Lore, Rupert Percy (ignotus)

Wildlife on Your Doorstep, Robert Gibbons (Reader's Digest)

Witches & Neighbours, Robin Briggs (HarperCollins)

The Witch's Treasury of the Countryside, Draco and Harriss (ignotus)

A Witch's Treasury of Hearth & Garden, Gabrielle Sidonie (ignotus)

Author biography

Writing as Mélusine Draco, the author has been a magical and spiritual instructor for over 20 years, and writer of numerous popular books including *Liber Agyptius: The Book of Egyptian Magic*; *The Hollow Tree*, an elementary guide to Qabalah; *A Witch's Treasury of the Countryside*; *Root & Branch: British Magical Tree Lore* and *Starchild: a rediscovery of stellar wisdom*. Her highly individualistic teaching methods, as used in *Traditional Witchcraft for Urban Living*, draw on historical sources, supported by academic texts and current archaeological findings.

MOON

BOOKS

Moon Books invites you to begin or deepen your encounter with Paganism, in all its rich, creative, flourishing forms.